Mary Downey FMA

KINDLE A FIRE

Retreats for Second-Level Schools

Behold, all you who kindle a fire...
Walk by the light of your fire.
Isaiah 50:11

VERITAS

First published 1995 by
Veritas Publications
7-8 Lower Abbey Street
Dublin 1

ISBN 1 85390 204 7

British Library Cataloguing
in Publication Data.
A catalogue record for
this book is available
from the British Library.

The author and publishers are grateful to the following for permission to reproduce their copyright material.

HarperCollins Publishers Inc., *Intimate Strangers: Men and Women Together*, Lillian B. Rubin. Copyright © 1983 by Lillian B. Rubin; selected excerpt from *The Gulag Archipelago 1918-1956: An experiment in Literary Investigation I-II by Aleksandr I. Solzhenitsyn.* Copyright © 1973 by Aleksandr I. Solzhenitsyn. English language translation copyright © 1973, 1974 by Harper & Row Publishers, Inc. Reprinted by permission of HarperCollins Publishers, Inc.; Anthony Clarke and Source Books, *Psalms of a Laywoman*, Edwina Gately; St Mary's Press, MN, *Dreams Alive: Prayers by Teenagers*, ed. Carl Koch, *Earthsongs*, Wayne Simsic; St Pauls, *More Parables and Fables*, Peter Ribes SJ; Mowbray, London, *By Way of the Heart*, Wilkie Au; Pan Macmillan, *Jonathan Livingston Seagull*, Richard Bach, *The Diary of Anne Frank*, Anne Frank; *The Irish Independent*, extract from edition of 19 July 1994; Zondervan Publishing, *A Step Further*, Joni Eareckson; Weidenfeld & Nicholson, *Under the Eye of the Clock*, Christopher Nolan; Kevin Mayhew Publishers, 'Do not be Afraid', Gerard Markland. Copyright © Kevin Mayhew Ltd. Reproduced by permission, licence number 592071; Weston Priory Productions, 'Hosea', from *The Rising of the Sun* (Book 2); Scriptures quoted from the *Good News Bible* published by The Bible Societies/HarperCollins Publishers Ltd, UK © American Bible Society, 1966, 1971, 1976, 1992, with permission. Gallery Press, 'Primrose', 'The Gift' and 'From Failure Up', Patrick Kavanagh. Concordia Publishing House, *Psalms Now*, Leslie F. Brandt.

Design: Bill Bolger
Printed in the Republic of Ireland by Betaprint Ltd

Contents

Juniors

Seniors

Introduction

In working both directly and indirectly with young people it became clear to me that while some may form no strong links with the institutional Church, their openness to and yearning for something spiritual is alive and well. This sense was confirmed when I tentatively began to explore creatively some spiritual themes with them. Thus, *Kindle a Fire* began to take shape. The title is significant. What can sometimes appear to be dry wood, cut off with little nourishment flowing through it from its roots, is waiting, perhaps without knowing it, for something or someone to bring it alive by connecting with it in a way that is relevant. I have seen fires being kindled and have known myself to be on 'holy ground' with a sense of deep reverence as God and the young person reached out to each other. *Kindle a Fire* is an invitation to become part of this experience.

The Retreats in Context

Kindle a Fire contains ten 'retreats' for young people in second-level schools or other areas of youth ministry. Five of these are for junior cycle and the first of these, 'Journeying with God – new beginnings', is specifically for first years. The other five retreats are designed for senior cycle or the older adolescent, and the second of these, 'Every common bush afire with God', which deals with endings and new beginnings, is particularly suited to sixth years or any other group in transition from the known to the less known.

The term 'retreat' could be confining. Each theme may be used whenever it is appropriate, either in the school year or in the lives of the young people themselves. Each retreat is a block of time – two to three hours – set aside so that they can prayerfully explore and celebrate a theme which they may have approached at a different level elsewhere. The time allotted to this experience can depend on the length of time the retreat facilitator decides to give to each activity. The whole approach invites people to 'go with the flow'. It isn't important to cover every aspect of what is suggested. The choice can depend on two things. Firstly, what the facilitator is comfortable doing – for example, not everyone may want to include the dance where this is suggested. Secondly, the choice can be related to what the pupils enjoy doing – colouring, writing, meditation – and more time can be given to these. The young people's response may then challenge us to explore other elements from which we shied away at first! Where facilitators wish to extend the time to a day, a theme could be worked through – perhaps a three-hour span – and be followed by preparation for the celebration of either the sacrament of Reconciliation or Eucharist.

Various Elements Used

1 Guided meditation

This is a sacred space for each young person. What happens within that space will be different for each individual and cannot be judged. However, it is important that it be followed by a time which is designed to help the students to reflect on the meditation, and that this can be a time which helps them to grow in their relationship with God, with others and with themselves. All but one of these meditations are to be found on *A Time to Pray* tapes 1, 2 & 3. However, as the scripts are provided here you may decide to read them yourself. To use this meditation time effectively I suggest the following:

1   Paper, pens, crayons… anything that is necessary for this time is best taken out or distributed prior to the meditation and placed near each student.
2   Briefly introduce the theme of the prayer.
3   Give instructions to the students regarding the written response which they will be required to make to the meditation so as not to break the link between the meditation and the response.

4 Play the tape or read the script against a background of reflective music.
5 As the meditation tape finishes play some reflective music.
6 Allow the students two or three minutes for reflection on their prayers before writing.
7 Ask the students to write their response.

2 Colouring

Because guided meditation and reflective prayer generally opens up the whole area of images in prayer some young people feel very much at home expressing these images through the medium of colour (crayons or markers are usually more facilitator-friendly than paint and all that painting involves). It is important to remember that these illustrations may have a story that won't be apparent to others and the unfolding of which could be invited by asking, 'Would you like to talk to me/us about your illustration?'

3 Small group sharing

Sharing in pairs or in small groups of four or five, when the pupils show signs of readiness for this, could create an atmosphere of trust and openness. While the material used in the retreat is personal to each one and needs to be respected as 'holy ground', there will be elements that they may feel comfortable sharing. It is an aspect that needs sensitive handling so that the pupils know when their responses are personal and private and when some sharing will be appropriate.

4 Dance

You may like to introduce the pupils to circular meditative dances which are very simple and fairly easy to get into. It is one way of allowing the pupils to see that we can pray with more than the mind! Given some time they quieten and enjoy this new prayerful experience. (For details on dance resources, see p.64.)

Preparation of the Room

The various elements of these retreats require that as much space as possible be allowed in the room. Chairs could be put in a large circle and, where possible, some cushions could be supplied for those who may want to sit on the floor. While all that is necessary as a focus for each retreat is a candle, the facilitator can add whatever he or she perceives to be appropriate, for example an icon, flowers, etc. What is of great importance is the atmosphere that is created. One suggestion is to play music as the young people begin to enter the room. It is important also that the facilitator will have provided everything on the list of 'things you will need', given before each retreat. This, too, communicates a relaxed atmosphere.

Kindle a Fire

In all of this what we are endeavouring to do is create a space in the pupils' lives where they may be more aware of the God who journeys with them in and through the bits and pieces of their day. Perhaps we too will get glimpses of his presence as we seek to 'kindle a fire', and may each one of us 'walk by the light of that fire' (Isaiah 50:11).

Note: Text in italic type denotes an instruction for the facilitator.

Handouts, which may be photocopied and distributed to the pupils, are indicated in the text by this symbol:

PHOTO
COPY

PHOTO
COPY

Journeying with God – new beginnings

Things you will need
- *copies of worksheet 'Baptism... Confirmation' (p.7)*
- *a tape of the song 'Holy, Sacred Spirit'*
- *a large candle*
- *copies of handout 'Me on my journey' (p.8)*
- *music for dance (optional)*
- *a tape of reflective music*
- *copies of handout 'God's message to me' (p.10)*
- *crayons*
- *art paper*

Introduction

Today we will be thinking and talking about our journey with God in our life. We began this journey years ago although we may not think about it very much. Baptism was a significant moment on that journey – one of the very first landmarks – and then, more recently, Confirmation became another important landmark.

Let us stop for a little while and think back on our journey from Baptism to Confirmation. *Play reflective music in the background.*

Handout

PHOTO COPY

PHOTO COPY

PHOTO COPY

PHOTO COPY

Worksheet

Baptism...
....
....
....
....

Confirmation..
....
....
....
....

Fill in the special landmarks that you remember on your journey from Baptism to Confirmation.
Spend some time reflecting on the people who were part of that landmark.
Why was it an important landmark?
What do you recall about yourself at that time?

Allow the pupils a quiet time to fill this in.

Sharing

Share briefly with the group.

Song

For a moment, think back on your Confirmation and, as you listen to and then sing the following chant, you will ask the Holy Spirit to be with you very specially on your journey.

'Holy, Sacred Spirit' (Monica Brown, *Remembering Heart*)

> Holy, Sacred Spirit
> Breathe your life in us (2)

Prayer

Light the candle. Read slowly:
I am the light of the world
Anyone who follows me will not be walking in the dark
but will have the light of life.

In your light we see light.

Anyone who claims to be in the light
but hates his brother or sister is still in the dark.
But anyone who loves his brother or sister is living in the light
and need not be afraid of stumbling;
unlike the person who hates his brother or sister and is in the darkness,
not knowing where he is going because it is too dark to see.

Extinguish the candle.
Sometimes we don't allow Jesus to be the light on our journey. We will spend a few minutes thinking of times when we walked in darkness:

....   When we were selfish
....   When we didn't respect ourselves, other people or creation around us
....   When we were lazy and didn't use our talents, our energy
....   When we weren't truthful
...   When....

In the quiet of our hearts let us now ask God to forgive us and to be with us on our journey.

Relight the candle.
We have relit the candle that will throw light on our journey.

First of all it gives us light to see ourselves – to see who we are now that we have journeyed from Baptism to Confirmation and are ready to move forward.

Distribute this handout.

Handout

Me on my journey

1. The time I feel most alive is...
2. The time I feel most alone is...
3. The words that describe how I see myself are...
4. The words that describe how my friends see me are...
5. My dream for the future is...
6. When I am with people whom I don't know I feel...
7. The person I admire most is...
8. The aspect of my life I would most like to change is...
9. I get mad when...
10. My greatest gift is...
11. When somebody praises me I feel...
12. It is hard for me when...

Allow the pupils a quiet time to complete the handout.
Ask the pupils to share whatever is appropriate with the person next to them.

Dance (Optional)

To show that we are ready to set out on our journey let's pretend that we have put on our pilgrim sandals and dance.

As we move in we remember that we are on a journey with God who lives within each of us. As we move out we remember that we are on a journey with all those around us and with all the people of the world.

Guided meditation

God's presence

Music – nature sounds etc.

1. As we begin these few moments of quiet and reflection try to relax and leave behind the tensions and anxieties of the day.

   Make sure that your body feels comfortable, your feet are on the floor, your back is in a relaxed position in your chair. If you wish, close your eyes. Become aware of your breathing. Imagine the breath of life reaching into each part of your body.

   Become aware of the sounds in the room and outside the room. Feel your body relax.

   Music

2. Sometimes God seems very distant and unreal.

   Sometimes we feel that God is close to us.

   Think of a time when you felt that God was very far away from you. Remember what it felt like.

   Think of a time when you felt close to God.

   Remember what that felt like.

   God, our Creator, help us to be aware that you are always present with us:
   that you breathe the breath of life through our bodies;
   that you hold us in the palm of your hand;
   that you have counted the hairs on our heads.

   Give us a sense of security in your presence, an awareness that we are loved by you at all times, that we are important to you, and that we can always turn to you, with confidence that you will be there waiting for us.
   Music

3. Imagine what it would be like if we really believed that God would take care of all our needs.

   Which of your needs would you like to present to God right now?

   Ask God for help or guidance in whichever area of your life you wish.

   Listen to what God is saying to you right now – something which has special meaning for your life today.
   Music

4. Become aware, again, of the sounds in the room, of the other people around you, as you listen to the music.
   You could finish with a song.

Reflection

Write these questions for personal reflection on the flip-chart or blackboard:

1. During the meditation what did you most need to hear God say to you? What was your response?

2. How do you imagine God who takes care of all our needs?
   What are your feelings about that?

3. How do you think you can become more aware of God's presence in the world and in your life?

Handout

God's message to me

This is God's message to you. Insert your own name in the spaces.

I made you, ..., in my own image and likeness
and when I made you I saw that you are good.
Before the world, ..., I chose you,
chose you in Christ, to be holy and spotless,
and to live through love in my presence.
I chose you, ..., to live with me.
You, ..., are my friend.
Do not be afraid, ..., for I have saved you.
I have called you by your name, ...
When you go through deep waters and great trouble,
I will be with you. When you go through rivers
of difficulty, you will not drown. When you walk
through the fire of suffering you will not be
burned up – the flames will not destroy you.
Do not be afraid, ..., for I am with you.
You are precious in my eyes, ...,
you are honoured and I love you.
You are always in my presence, ...,
and I hold you by your right hand.
Now I will guide you with advice,
and in the end receive you into glory.
Christ is in you, ..., your hope and glory.

With reflective music in background allow the pupils time to pray this message to themselves.

Which of these sentences is your favourite? Why?

Sharing

God's presence in my life's journey

Illustrate this theme using:
- colour
- poem
- story
- other

Each person shows or reads his or her illustration to the group.

Path in life

Make a path around the candle with the illustrations, etc.
Ask the pupils to walk quietly on the path and to see how the others express God's presence on their journey in life.

Take time to ask God to allow us to be more aware of his presence as we walk with him in life. This may be done in the form of a letter or a quiet prayer.

Sharing life with others

Things you will need
- *copies of the questions on*
  The Little Prince *(p.12)*
- *reflective music*
- *crayons*
- *art paper*
- *copies of the handout
  'Prayers of young people'
  (pp.13-14)*
- *copies of 'A Letter from
  Jesus' (p.15)*
- *a tape of the song 'Love is
  the greatest gift of all'
  (Monica Browne,
  Celebrating our Journey)*

Introduction

Imagine that you are about to go on a journey around the world. Make a list of eight things which you would consider to be very important to take with you. Make out this list in order of importance and give your reasons for each choice.

Feedback
- Give examples of what you listed 1, 2 and 3.
- Are your family and friends listed? Why? Why not?

Read this extract from The Little Prince *to the pupils.*

Story
Establishing ties

It was then that the fox appeared.
'Good morning,' said the fox.
'Good morning,' the little prince responded politely,
although when he turned around he saw nothing.
'I am right here,' the voice said, 'under the apple tree.'
'Who are you?' asked the little prince, and added,
'You are very pretty to look at.'
'I am a fox,' the fox said.
'Come and play with me,' proposed the little prince. 'I am so unhappy.'
'I cannot play with you,' the fox said. 'I am not tamed.'
'Ah! Please excuse me,' said the little prince.
But, after some thought, he added,
'What does that mean – "tame"?'
'You do not live here,' said the fox. 'What is it that you are looking for?'
'I am looking for me,' said the little prince. 'What does that mean – "tame"?'
'Men,' said the fox. 'They have guns, and they hunt. It is very disturbing. They also raise chickens. These are their only interests. Are you looking for chickens?'
'No,' said the little prince. 'I am looking for friends. What does that mean – "tame"?'
'It is an act often neglected,' said the fox. 'It means to establish ties.'
'To establish ties'?
'Just that,' said the fox. 'To me, you are still nothing more than a little boy who is just like a hundred thousand other little boys. And I have no need of you. And you, on your part, have no need of me. To you, I am nothing more than a fox like a hundred thousand other foxes. But if you tame me, then we shall need each other. To me, you will be unique in all the world. To you, I shall be unique in all the world...'

'My life is very monotonous,' he said. 'I hunt chickens; men hunt me. All the chickens are just alike, and all the men are just alike. And, in consequence, I am a little bored. But if you tame me, it will be as if the sun came to shine on my life. I shall know the sound of a step that will be different from all the others. Other steps send me hurrying back underneath the ground. Yours will call me, like music, out of my burrow. And then look: you see the grain-fields down yonder? I do not eat bread. Wheat is of no use to me. The wheat fields have nothing to say to me. And that is sad. But you have hair that is the colour of gold. Think how wonderful that will be when you have tamed me! The grain, which is also golden, will bring me back the thought of you. And I shall love to listen to the wind in the wheat...'

The fox gazed at the little prince, for a long time.

'Please – tame me!' he said.

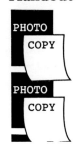

Handout

Answer these questions personally:

1. Make a list of the people who have 'tamed you', people with whom you have 'established ties'.
2. The fox said that establishing ties with people is 'an act too often neglected'. Why do you think people don't make friends?
3. What do you think it is like to be 'unique in all the world'?
   Have you ever experienced this?
4. This extract is saying some very important things about friendship. What are they?

Sharing

Share in small groups on whatever the pupils feel comfortable sharing, especially from questions 2, 3 and 4.

Guided meditation

Close your eyes or focus on the candle. Become aware of the rhythm of your breathing. Don't change it, just become aware of it. Become aware of the stillness of the room. For a moment thank God for the gift of this new day, for the gift of life and energy. Become aware of your own space in this room, a room which you share with others and where you have your own space.

Now, in your imagination go to a country road. As you walk along this country road you begin to sense in yourself that you would like to explore. You find a gate leading into a field and you walk freely across this field and another and another until finally you arrive at a riverbank. As you stand there you begin to realise that it is the river of your life. What are your thoughts and feelings as you look at this river?

Slowly you return upstream along the river of your life to where it all began – the source to which you are still vitally connected today. Jesus is sitting beside the river and invites you to sit beside him. You look into the still deep water and you think of the people who helped to form the reflection you now see of yourself, those people who, like water, were natural, deep, life-giving. You think of your parents who gave you life and nourishment, who helped you to discover what is best in yourself. Brothers and sisters also helped to form you into the reflection that looks back at you from the water. Spend some time thanking God for the gift of home and family.

Like any river, many streams join it on its course, adding their own refreshing waters – yet becoming one with the main river. Recall those 'streams' – those other people outside the family who were also of influence in making your reflection what it is today – neighbours, relatives, friends, special friends along your life's journey. In becoming aware of what you have received from them give thanks to the God of life.

As you sit there beside Jesus you think of the present moment where you are now in the river of your life. You think of the people who are important in your life – the gift that they are in your life – the gift that you are in their life. And you give thanks to God.

Then Jesus says to you 'I will be there with you as the river of your life flows on. Trust me to be always with you'. You stay quietly with Jesus, content to be in his presence beside the river of your life.

As you leave the river bank and begin your journey back you recall Jesus telling you that he will always be with you.

When you are ready open your eyes.

Colouring
Illustrate (using crayons) what this meditation said to you.

Sharing
Share a brief word with the group about your illustration.

Handout   *Distribute this handout.*

Dear God,

It seems lately that I've been having a hard time making new friends. If you could, please give me the strength and courage to make it through each day with my head up high and without getting depressed and frustrated with myself. I know it takes time to make new friends, but I am very impatient and excited about making new friends. Help and guide me through each day to bring happiness to someone's day.

Dear God,

We have reached a difficult time in our life. The world we live in is very demanding. We need your help and guidance to find the path we should follow. Please help us to remember the important things in life: family, friendship, prayer, love and relationships. Never let us get so caught up in material goods that we forget to see the beauty in a sunset and the worth of a smile. Amen.

Dear God,

As I walk through the halls at school,
I notice the familiar faces
of those I call my friends.

They can put me in a good mood
with a friendly smile
or just a simple 'hello'.
I'm thankful for my friends, God,
because they make me feel that I'm important;
I feel as if I'm needed
when a friend comes to me with a problem.

Please help me to be a true friend to others
and to give back to them,
through friendship,
what they have given to me.

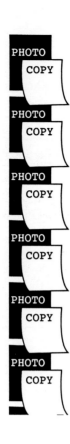

So many times I get so caught up in schoolwork and activities that I forget the most important things in life, which are family and friends. Help me to take time out of my busy life schedule to spend quality time with the people who are most important to me, in order to let them know that they are special and a vital part of my life. Let me always be sensitive to their feelings so that I may be a better friend. Amen.

Today I acknowledge the joy that friends bring into my life. I give thanks to God for the friends with whom I share joy, laughter, companionship, comfort, and understanding. Thanks for my friends who welcome me, who make me feel comfortable in just being me. I think of myself as a friend to all, reaching out and welcoming. I can reach out to others by showing a sincere interest in them. Thank you, God, for making me feel welcome in you. Help me to make others feel welcome too. Amen.

Dreams Alive, Prayers by Teenagers
Ed. Carl Koch

- Pick out the most important points in each of these letters and list them.
- Why do you think each of these points is important?
- What would you like to say to the person who made this point in her or his letter?

Share the answers to these questions either in your class group or in pairs.

Story
The Cobbler
One night in his sleep, an old cobbler heard a voice. The voice told him that on the next day the Lord Jesus would come to visit him. The next morning he began the day with a feeling that something wonderful was about to happen. He wondered when the important visitor whom he awaited would arrive. And he did have some visitors during the day: first there was an old beggar, thin and worn looking with tattered clothes and a tearing cough. The old cobbler took him in, warmed him by the fire and gave him food. Then came a woman, thin for want of food and frozen with the cold, carrying her baby in her arms. She asked for food and clothing and the old cobbler gave her what he could. Then next to arrive at the cobbler's door was an apple woman who was very upset because a boy had tried to steal her apples. The cobbler knew who this boy was and brought the two together and reconciled them.

At the end of the day the cobbler was still waiting for the Lord's visit. Though he was tired he didn't go to bed but soon he fell asleep on his chair by the fire, still wondering when the Lord would come. As he slept he heard the same voice as he had heard the previous night. 'I was hungry and you fed me. I was thirsty and you gave me drink. I was sick and you nourished me.'

Play reflective music and ask these questions on the theme of 'Myself as friend'.
- Are there ways in which you can be like the cobbler?
- What does Jesus say to you?
- Where did you meet Christ today:
  In someone at home who needed a kind word or helping hand?
  In a friend who needed someone to talk to when things were difficult?
  In a group in the neighourhood where you live who need support?
- Perhaps as you thought about these questions you felt you could have been a better friend at times.
  For these times let us quietly ask God to forgive us.

14

Reflection

Handout

Distribute copies of this 'letter from Jesus'.
Insert your own name in the space after 'Dear....'

Dear..........,

From before time began you have been loved. I love you. My life and death showed my great love for you. Because I love you I want you to trust me – one step, one day at a time. Knowing that you are special to me will make you free. Be yourself! I will be at your side guiding you if you allow me to do so. Be aware of my presence in everything. I am like a shepherd to you, leading you safely through difficult times as well as good.... I have always provided for you. Because I love you, please love yourself and love others also. There are so many people in the world who have never known what it is like to love or be loved. Will you share my love in friendship with others? It is in loving that we become most truly ourselves. The world would be such a different place if everyone shared friendship with each other.

Your friend,
Jesus

With quiet music playing in the background allow some quiet time for the pupils to answer this letter.

Sharing

Ask the pupils to share on these questions:
* What was it like for you to read this letter from Jesus?
* What was the part of it that meant most to you? Why?
* Would you like to say one thing that you said to Jesus?

Allow the pupils a quiet time to pray their letter to Jesus.

Concluding song

'Love is the greatest gift of all' (Monica Brown, *Celebrating our Journey*)

I love you this much

Things you will need
- *copies of the song 'Come back to me' (pp.16-17)*
- *a tape of reflective music*
- *copies of questions on the meditation (p.18)*
- *copies of scripture passages (pp.18-20)*
- *a large candle*
- *small candles – one for each pupil*
- *a tape of the Taizé chant, 'Jesus remember me' (Laudate)*
- *crayons*
- *art paper*
- *a fairly large cross*
- *copies of the song 'Remembering heart'*

Introduction

Ours is a world of mass communication. We can telephone family or friends from one end of the world to the other. We can switch on the TV and hear the latest news, again, from any part of the world. These means of communication can make the world seem like a global village. Here at home we hear a lot of talk about communication – in fact, people do training courses in communications skills. When it comes to the way we relate with people good communication is at the very heart of it. We all feel the need of being listened to – really listened to. When it comes to revealing who we really are to the other person we come in touch with a lot of feelings within ourselves. We can sometimes want to share all our thoughts and feelings with at least one significant person. It is easy? This is how one person – let's call her Ann – experienced it.

Talking about it this way makes me realise that it's not so simple as I'm saying. Actually, I have to admit that it's a double-edged thing. It's hard to explain, but sometimes I feel a real safe feeling in the fact that he doesn't notice what's happening with me. That way what I'm feeling and thinking is only up for notice and discussion if I bring it up. There's a way it feels safer even though there's also a kind of loneliness about it. It means it's all up to me to have it on the agenda. If I don't bring it up, forget it, Lloyd's certainly not going to. So, like I said, it works both ways; it's got its good points and bad ones. But one thing's sure, I can hide myself as much as I need to.
Intimate Strangers, Lillian B. Rubin

Sharing

Share in pairs
Write questions on the blackboard or flip-chart.
1   What does this extract tell you about Ann?
2   What does it tell you about communication?
3   Have you read novels or seen films where a similar situation occurs, that is, questions and difficulties about revealing our feelings?
    (Remains of the Day *and* Shadowlands *are two such films which could be mentioned here.*)

Handout

PHOTO COPY

Song

Distribute copies of the words of this song.
Hosea

Come back to me with all your heart
Don't let fear keep us apart

Trees do bend though straight and tall
So much we to others call.

Long have I waited for your coming home to me
And living deeply our new life.
The wilderness will lead you
To your heart where I will speak
Integrity and justice
With tenderness you shall know.

You shall sleep secure with peace
Faithfulness will be your joy.

Two words that stand out for me in this song are:
HEART and FEAR.

What is the risk of loving people and allowing them to know that we love them?

Brainstorm
When you hear the word 'LENT' what words come quickly to your mind?
Record the words on the blackboard or flip-chart.

Do you ever think of Lent as a time to reflect:
- on a love story?
- on God's special love for us?
- on the fact that Jesus risked so much in communicating his love for each one of us... to the point that he gave his life for us?

Guided meditation
A journey into suffering
Close your eyes or focus on the candle.

Become aware of your breathing. Notice it – don't change it. As you breathe in let your breath fill your body... your head... chest... all your body. Notice how you feel at the end of this. Share it with the Lord.

Once again pay attention to your breathing. As you breathe in you are breathing in God's love. As you breathe in say the word 'love'.

We want to thank God for the gift of life that flows through us... for the gifts we have received today. Let us breathe out our thanks. Stay with that rhythm – breathing in 'love', breathing out 'thanks'.

Imagine it is early evening and that you are on a journey along a dirt road going towards Jerusalem. In the distance you can see the city outlined against the sky... its towers and stone buildings and all of it surrounded by an enormous wall. There are other people on the road. In particular you notice a group of men just ahead of you. You notice that it is quiet here but you sense that it is an eerie quiet, as though something important is about to happen.

The man at the centre of the group draws apart from the others and you find yourself walking alongside him. You look at this man... this man of Galilee with his eyes turned towards Jerusalem. His steps become slower as you walk together in silence. You sense that he carries an enormous burden as you notice various strong emotions in his facial expression. You sense fear – fear of future suffering. You sense a profound fear of being abandoned... of being left alone. You see indecision... a struggle to accept what is about to happen. Then Jesus becomes aware that you walk beside him. You allow Jesus to speak to you personally of what he is experiencing at this time...

Become aware of your own thoughts, your own feelings as you listen to Jesus. He invites you to share these thoughts and feelings with him...

Together you continue your journey along the dirt road. But now you have both become silent again. You think your thoughts of Jesus' suffering – suffering that will lead to death on a cross. You think of suffering as you see it in today's world. You think of suffering as you experience it yourself. Together we look at a God who chose poverty, weakness and suffering...

Soon you notice that your journey together has led you to the entrance into a garden, an entrance lined by olive trees. The men who had accompanied Jesus before he drew aside are already there. You stand at the entrance to the garden and you watch as Jesus approaches his disciples. Be aware of your thoughts, be aware of your feelings. Become aware once again of your breathing. As you inhale you once again say 'love' and as you exhale you say 'thanks'.

When you are ready open your eyes.

Reflection

Distribute copies of these questions and ask the pupils to reflect privately on them.
Play reflective music in the background.

Handout

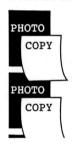

1. Jesus shares with you what he is experiencing at this time and then invites you to tell him your thoughts and feelings.
    Write your response.
2. Can you identify with Jesus when he speaks to you about
    – needing support?
    – a special friend betraying you?
    – feeling a failure?
    Does it help you to come closer to Jesus?

Sharing

Share in twos or threes.
Share only what you feel comfortable sharing.

Becoming part of the journey to Calvary

Handout

Luke 22

And he came out, and went, as was his custom, to the Mount of Olives; and the disciples followed him. And when he came to the place he said to them, 'Pray that you may not enter into temptation'. And he withdrew from them about a stone's throw, and knelt down and prayed, 'Father, if thou art willing, remove this cup from me; nevertheless not my will, but thine, be done'. And there appeared to him an angel from heaven, strengthening him. And being in an agony he prayed more earnestly; and his sweat became like great drops of blood falling down upon the ground. And when he rose from prayer, he came to the disciples and found them sleeping for sorrow, and he said to them, 'Why do you sleep? Rise and pray that you may not enter into temptation'.

What does this passage say to you
    – about Jesus?
    – about suffering?

Note your thoughts and your feelings as you stay quietly with the passage.

18

Luke 22

Then they seized him and led him away, bringing him into the high priest's house. Peter followed at a distance; and when they had kindled a fire in the middle of the courtyard and sat down together, Peter sat among them. Then a maid, seeing him as he sat in the light and gazing at him said, 'This man also was with him'. But he denied it, saying, 'Woman, I do not know him'. And a little later someone else saw him and said, 'You also are one of them'. But Peter said, 'Man, I am not'. And after an interval of about an hour still another insisted, saying, 'Certainly this man also was with him; for he is a Galilean'. But Peter said, 'Man, I do not know what you are saying'. And immediately, while he was still speaking, the cock crowed. And the Lord turned and looked at Peter. And Peter remembered the word of the Lord, how he had said to him, 'Before the cock crows today, you will deny me three times'. And he went out and wept bitterly.

What does this passage say to you
- about Jesus?
- about suffering?

Note your thoughts and your feelings as you stay quietly with the passage.

Mark 14

And they went to a place which was called Gethsemane; and he said to his disciples, 'Sit here, while I pray'. And he took with him Peter and James and John, and began to be greatly distressed and troubled. And he said to them, 'My soul is very sorrowful, even to death; remain here, and watch'. And going a little farther, he fell on the ground and prayed that, if it were possible, the hour might pass from him. And he said, 'Abba, Father, all things are possible to thee; remove this cup from me; yet not what I will, but what thou wilt'. And he came and found them sleeping, and he said to Peter, 'Simon, are you asleep? Could you not watch one hour? Watch and pray that you may not enter into temptation; the spirit indeed is willing, but the flesh is weak'. And again he went away and prayed, saying the same words. And again he came and found them sleeping, for their eyes were very heavy; and they did not know what to answer him. And he came the third time, and said to them, 'Are you still sleeping and taking your rest? It is enough; the hour has come; the Son of man is betrayed into the hands of sinners. Rise, let us be going; see, my betrayer is at hand'.

What does this passage say to you
- about Jesus?
- about suffering?

Note your thoughts and your feelings as you stay quietly with the passage.

Mark 15

And they compelled a passer-by, Simon of Cyrene, who was coming in from the country, the father of Alexander and Rufus, to carry his cross. And they brought him to the place called Golgotha (which means the place of a skull). And they offered him wine mingled with myrrh; but he did not take it. And they crucified him, and divided his garments among them, casting lots for them, to decide what each should take. And it was the third hour, when they crucified him. And the inscription of the charge against him read, 'The King of the Jews'. And with him they crucified two robbers, one on his right and one on his left. And those who passed by derided him, wagging their heads,

19

and saying, 'Aha! You who would destroy the Temple and build it in three days, save yourself, and come down from the cross!' So also the chief priests mocked him to one another with the scribes, saying, 'He saved others; he cannot save himself. Let the Christ, the King of Israel, come down now from the cross, that we may see and believe'. Those who were crucified with him also reviled him.

What does this passage say to you
— about Jesus?
— about suffering?

Note your thoughts and your feelings as you stay quietly with the passage.

Mark 15

And when the sixth hour had come, there was darkness over the whole land until the ninth hour. And at the ninth hour Jesus cried with a loud voice, 'Eloi, Eloi, lama sabachthani?' which means, 'My God, my God, why hast thou forsaken me?' And some of the bystanders hearing it said, 'Behold, he is calling Elijah'. And one ran and, filling a sponge full of vinegar, put it on a reed and gave it to him to drink, saying, 'Wait, let us see whether Elijah will come to take him down'. And Jesus uttered a loud cry, and breathed his last. And the curtain of the temple was torn in two, from top to bottom. And when the centurion, who stood facing him, saw that he thus breathed his last, he said, 'Truly this man was the Son of God!'.

What does this passage say to you
— about Jesus?
— about suffering?

Note your thoughts and your feelings as you stay quietly with the passage.

Luke 22

While he was still speaking, there came a crowd, and the man called Judas, one of the twelve, was leading them. He drew near to Jesus to kiss him; but Jesus said to him, 'Judas, would you betray the Son of man with a kiss?' And when those who were about him saw what would follow, they said, 'Lord, shall we strike with the sword?' And one of them struck the slave of the high priest and cut off his right ear. But Jesus said, 'No more of this!' And he touched his ear and healed him. Then Jesus said to the chief priests and captains of the Temple and elders, who had come out against him, 'Have you come out as against a robber, with swords and clubs? When I was with you day after day in the Temple, you did not lay hands on me. But this is your hour, and power of darkness'.

What does this passage say to you
— about Jesus?
— about suffering?

Note your thoughts and your feelings as you stay quietly with the passage.

Each pupil takes a copy of one of the scripture passages – a section of this road to suffering and death.

Ask them to spend some time quietly with the passage. Ask them:
What does this passage say to you
– about Jesus?
– about suffering?

Note your thoughts and feelings as you stay quietly with this passage.

In her or his own time each person will come forward, light a candle and place it in a circle around the wood of the cross. Each person will say a word on what the reflection said to her or him.

Song

'Jesus Remember Me' (Taizé, *Laudate*)

Guided reflection

I remember seeing a poster that had the question
'Lord, how much do you love me?'
printed on it. The answer went something like:
'I love you this much', and he opened his arms and died.

As we think of this kind of love – of a friend who loved us enough to die for us – what image or images come to us
   – of love?
   – of love that challenges us?
   – of responding to this love?

Allow the pupils time to illustrate their images with music playing in background.

Ask the pupils to:
•   share a brief word about the image or images that came to them
•   put their images near the cross

Concluding song

'Remembering Heart' (Monica Brown, *Remembering Heart)*

A journey in Advent

Things you will need
- *art paper*
- *pencils and biros*
- *crayons*
- *clay*
- *a tape recorder*
- *a tape of soft music*
- *a tape of the song* 'When a Child is Born'
- *newspaper cuttings (recent) illustrating what appears to be important to people around Christmas*
- *candle and matches*
- *copies of the readings for the Sundays of Advent (pp.28-32)*
- *a rucksack*

While this retreat could be done with any age-group at second-level it is probably most suited to junior cycle. It combines the scriptural aspect of Advent with the personal accompaniment of Mary during her Advent, and then moves on to the challenge of personal preparation for Christmas.

One of the elements of this retreat is the family tree of Jesus of Nazareth. It is suggested that at one end of the room where the retreat is to take place there will be placed a 'tree trunk' and at the other end of the room an empty crib. The chairs for the pupils will be placed in a circle around the room. 'Branches' cut from strips of paper will also be needed and printed with names such as Abraham, Ruth, David.

Introduction

- *Show the pupils newspaper cuttings illustrating how people think about Christmas today. Read two or three of these.*
  Brainstorm the pupils on the words they would associate with Christmas, e.g.:
  – shopping
  – cooking
  – presents
- People have different ways of looking at things. For example, some of us could go for a walk and not be very aware of our surroundings. Perhaps the following story shows us how blind we can be, how we can become so caught up in everyday activities and anxieties that we may no longer notice the beauty around us ... beauty in things that we can take so much for granted. This is an extract from a book by Alexander Solzhenitsyn who writes of his experience as a prisoner. *(This extract may not be suitable for junior classes. If not, read the opening passage of* I am David, *by Anne Holm.)*

Story

Nonetheless, on clear days, above this muzzle, from the wall of the Lubyanka courtyard, from some windowpane or other on the sixth or seventh floor, we now and then got a pale reflection of a ray of sunlight. To us it was a real ray of sunlight – a living, dear being! We followed with affection its climb up the wall. And every step it made was filled with meaning, presaging the time of our daily outing in the fresh air, counting off several half-hours before lunch. Then, just before lunch, it disappeared.

And our rights included being let out for a walk, reading books, telling one another about the past, listening and learning, arguing and being educated! And we would be rewarded by a lunch that included two courses! Too good to be true!

The walk was bad on the first three floors of the Lubyanka. The prisoners were let out into a damp, low-lying little courtyard – the bottom of a narrow well between the prison buildings. But the prisoners on the fourth and fifth floors, on the other hand, were taken to an eagle's perch – on the roof of the fifth floor. It had a concrete floor; there were concrete walls three times the height of a man; we were accompanied by an unarmed jailer; on the watch tower was a sentinel with an automatic weapon. But the air was real and the sky was real! 'Hands behind your back! Line up in pairs! No talking! No stopping!' Such were the commands, but they forgot to forbid us to throw back our heads. And, of course, we did just that. Here one could see not a reflected, not a secondhand Sun, but the real one! The real, eternally living Sun itself! Or its golden diffusion through the spring clouds.

Spring promises everyone happiness – and tenfold to the prisoner. Oh, April sky! It didn't matter that I was in prison. Evidently, they were not going to shoot me. And in the end I would become wiser here. I would come to understand many things here, Heaven! I would correct my mistakes yet, O Heaven, not for them but for you, Heaven! I had come to understand those mistakes here, and I would correct them!

The Gulag Archipelago

What does this story say to you?

That there are different ways of looking at the same reality.

This is true also of ADVENT.

What is this extract saying to you:

– about Solzhenitsyn?

– about you?

– about us?

Advent is the four weeks coming up to Christmas. What words would you associate with Advent which are different from the words we connected with our newspaper cuttings?

– preparation

– waiting

– longing

Today we are are going on a journey in Advent.

Our starting-point, as we gather round this tree trunk, is the family tree of Jesus.

Place 'roots' with familiar names coming out from beneath the tree trunk.

These are some of the branches of Jesus' family tree and they go back over the centuries before he was born. As we know, they too were expecting the birth of a Messiah, so, like us at this time of year, they were preparing for his birth.

There is a song that could unite us with all these great people.

Song
'Prepare ye the way of the Lord' (*Godspell*)

Light the candle.

As we light this candle we pray that God will help us to prepare in a very special way this year for the birth of Jesus, his Son.

Mary and Joseph
Read St Matthew's account of Jesus' family tree, ending with 'And Jacob was the father of Joseph, the husband of Mary, of whom Jesus was born, who is called Christ'. *(Place Banners with the names Joseph and Mary written on them among the others at the base of the tree.)*

Dance (Optional)
We are now on a journey in the company of Mary, Joseph and other members of Jesus' family tree. To help us to experience that we are on a journey let us show this in dance.

Guided meditation

Sharing an Advent journey

All the people in Jesus' family tree were waiting. We are at the starting-point of our journey and I think it is time for us to ask one of Jesus' family to share her Advent journey with us.

Close your eyes or focus on the candle.

As you relax become aware of your breathing, in and out, in and out. Your steady breathing, your gift of life... Slowly become aware of the quietness of the room... the noises outside...

In your imagination go to a quiet country road. It is a December day, clear and cold. Sense the cold air on your hands and face. Become aware of the sounds around you on this country road. As you walk along you think of Christmas.
What are your thoughts?
What are your feelings?
Stay with these thoughts and feelings.

Gradually you realise that, lost in thought, you were hardly aware that the road you walked on had led into a wood. You become aware of the trees – many different kinds of trees – and you begin to wonder about their story: how long they have been growing there, how far down their roots go, what their story is...

And there, sitting by a special tree, is a woman. She looks up as you approach and waits to see if you want to come close to her. As she smiles at you you know it is Mary of Nazareth. She holds out her hand to you in welcome and as you sit down beside her in the wood she begins to speak to you. 'I come here often to my family tree', she tells you. 'I like to remember all those who waited for the birth of my Son, Jesus. They longed for him, you know. How they longed for his coming'.

As you sit listening to Mary you begin to see that the road you walk in Advent has footprints on it which are hundreds of years old and you find yourself asking these other travellers to share their deep longing for the birth of Jesus with you. Mary sits quietly beside you and knows your thoughts and longings.

Slowly you turn to Mary and you ask her how she felt the first time she travelled this Advent road. She smiles rather sadly and says: 'Thank you for asking. This special time for me, for all of us... goes unnoticed by so many. People are so busy with so many things at this time that they seem to travel by a different road and they don't seem to share my story'. Then she tells you what the Advent journey was like for her that first time...

'I waited', she said 'and I spoke to my unborn child of my waiting and longing for his coming.'

Soon you, too, begin to speak to the unborn Jesus of your waiting and your longing for his coming.

All too soon it is time for you to retrace your steps along the country road. As you do so, you know that Mary is beside you sharing the journey. Slowly you come back along the road and you notice once again how quiet it is. You notice once more that it is December and that the day is cold and clear. And you know that you are on a journey.

When you are ready open your eyes gently and focus on the candle.

Reflection
In this quiet time think of each of the following and write your response to the questions:
- What was it like for you to listen to Mary as she told you about waiting for the birth of Jesus? What were some of the things she shared with you?
- What are your thoughts and feelings now as you wait for Jesus' birth at Christmas?
- Do you think you would like to listen to and speak often to Mary who was a woman and a mother?

Signposts
I would like each of you at this point to begin to look out for signposts on our Advent journey. Perhaps we could do with a map to direct our feet to Christmas. Beside the tree trunk you will find a rucksack and inside this there is a map for each one of you.

Each pupil takes a 'map' – that is, a reading of one of the Sundays of Advent (pp.30-34). Ask them to read the 'map' quietly, asking themselves:

- What is this saying to me about Advent?

- What direction is it giving me personally by which to travel this Advent?

- What image comes to me to describe the direction I got from my reading?

Colouring
Ask the pupils to illustrate the image, using art paper and crayons.

Sharing
Share in twos or threes.
Share on these questions on 'Signposts' and on your image.

In the class group:
- Show your illustration
- Provide a word to accompany the illustration

A pathway in Advent
Place your illustrations one after another leading out from the tree trunk and forming a path.

Our destination
We are travelling along this path and our destination is an empty crib. Others have travelled this way before us, including some wise people.

Song
'When a Child is Born', Johnny Mathis

Scripture
Other travellers who brought gifts
Now when Jesus was born in Bethlehem of Judea in the days of Herod the king, behold, wise men from the East came to Jerusalem, saying, 'Where is he who has been born king of the Jews? For we have seen his star in the East, and have come to worship him'. When Herod the king heard this, he was troubled, and all Jerusalem with him; and assembling all the chief priests and scribes of the people, he inquired of them where the Christ was to be born. They told him, 'In Bethlehem of Judea; for so it is written by the prophet: 'And you, O Bethlehem, in the land of Judah, are by no means least among the rulers of Judah; for from you shall come a ruler who will govern my people Israel'.

Then Herod summoned the wise men secretly and ascertained from them what time the star appeared; and he sent them to Bethlehem, saying, 'Go and search diligently for the child, and when you have found him bring me word, that I too may come and worship him'. When they had heard the king they went their way; and lo, the star which they had seen in the East went before them, till it came to rest over the place where the child was. When they saw the star, they rejoiced exceedingly with great joy; and going into the house they saw the child with Mary his mother, and they fell down and worshipped him. Then, opening their treasures, they offered him gifts, gold and frankincense and myrrh. And being warned in a dream not to return to Herod, they departed to their own country by another way.

These wise people as we have heard carried gifts on their journey to Bethlehem for the new-born king.

Story

This lovely story by OHenry tells of the importance of choosing gifts, particularly at Christmas time.

The Christmas Gift

Tomorrow would be Christmas Day, and she had only $1.87 with which to buy Jim a present. She had been saving every penny she could for months, with this result.... Suddenly she whirled from the window and stood before the glass. Her eyes were shining brilliantly, but her face had lost its colour within twenty seconds.... Now, there were two possessions of the James Dillingham Youngs in which they both took a mighty pride. One was Jim's gold watch that had been his father's and his grandfather's. The other was Della's hair.... Della's hair fell about her, rippling and shining like a cascade of brown water. It reached below her knee and made itself almost a garment for her....

On went her old brown jacket; on went her old brown hat. With a whirl of skirts and with the brilliant sparkle still in her eyes, she fluttered out of the door and down the stairs to the street. Where she stopped the sign read: 'Mme Sofronie. Hair Goods of All Kinds.' One flight up Della ran, and collected herself, panting. Madame, large, too white, chilly, hardly looked the 'Sofronie'.

'Will you buy my hair?' asked Della.
'I buy hair,' said Madame. 'Take yer hat off and let's have a sight at the looks of it.'
Down rippled the brown cascade.
'Twenty dollars,' said Madame, lifting the mass with a practised hand.
'Give it to me quick', said Della.

Oh, and the next two hours tripped on rosy wings.... She was ransacking the stores for Jim's present. She found it at last. It surely had been made for him and no one else. There was no other like it in any of the stores, and she had turned all of them inside out. It was a platinum fob chain, simple and chaste in design, properly proclaiming its value by substance alone and not by meretricious ornamentation – as all good things should do. It was even worthy of The Watch. As soon as she saw it she knew that it must be Jim's. It was like him....

When Della reached home she got out her curling irons and lighted the gas and went to work repairing the ravages made by generosity added to love.... Within forty minutes her head was covered with tiny, close-lying curls that made her look wonderfully like a truant schoolboy....

Jim was never late. Della doubled the fob chain in her hand and sat on the corner of the table near the door that he always entered. Then she heard his step on the stair away down on the first flight, and she turned white for just a moment.... The door opened and Jim stepped in and closed it.... His eyes were fixed upon Della, and there was an expression in them that she could not read, and it terrified her.... 'Jim, darling!' she cried, 'don't look at me that way. I had my hair cut off and sold it because I couldn't have lived through Christmas without giving you a present. It'll grow again – you won't mind, will you? I just had to do it. My hair grows awfully fast. Merry Christmas! Jim, and let's be happy. You don't know what a nice – what a beautiful, nice gift I've got for you.'

Jim drew a package from his overcoat pocket and threw it upon the table. 'Don't make any mistake Dell,' he said, 'about me. I don't think there's anything in the way of a haircut or a shave or shampoo that could make me like my girl any less. But if you'll unwrap that package you may see why you had me going awhile at first.'

White fingers and nimble tore at the string and paper.... There lay The Combs – the set of combs, side and back, that Della had worshipped for long in a Broadway window. Beautiful combs, pure tortoiseshell, with jewelled rims – just the shade to wear in the beautiful vanished hair. They were expensive combs, she knew, and her heart had simply craved and yearned over them without the least hope of possession. And now they were hers. But the tresses that should have adorned the coveted adornments were gone.

Jim had not yet seen his beautiful present. She held it out to him eagerly upon her open palm. The dull precious metal seemed to flash with a reflection of her bright and ardent spirit. 'Isn't it dandy, Jim? I hunted all over town to find it. You'll have to look at the time a hundred times a day now. Give me your watch. I want to see how it looks on it.'

Instead of obeying, Jim tumbled down on the couch and put his hands under the back of his head and smiled. 'Dell', said he, 'let's put our Christmas presents away and keep 'em awhile. They're too nice to use just at present. I sold the watch to get the money to buy your combs. And now suppose you put the chops on.'

O Henry

Spend some time quietly making a clay symbol of the gift you think it would be appropriate for you to bring to Jesus this Christmas. As you create this symbol speak to Mary in your heart remembering the preparation she must have made for his coming on the first Christmas.

Share whatever you would like in the group about your symbol or anything else that struck you during this retreat.

Talk to Jesus about the gifts you would like to receive from him this Christmas.

Concluding hymns
In conclusion the pupils could sing some Christmas carols.

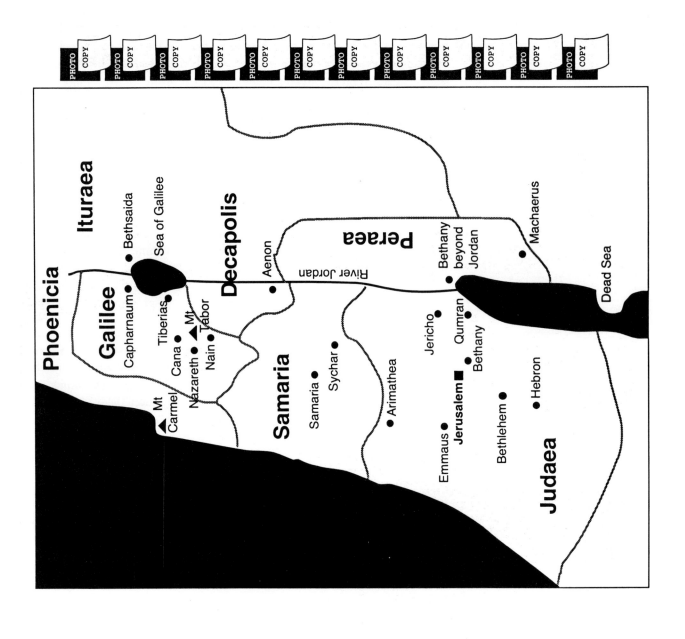

Old Testament Reading: Isaiah 11:1-10

He judges the wretched with integrity.

A shoot springs from the stock of Jesse,
a scion thrusts from his roots:
on him the spirit of the Lord rests,
a spirit of wisdom and insight,
a spirit of counsel and power,
a spirit of knowledge and of the fear of the Lord.
(The fear of the Lord is his breath.)
He does not judge by appearances,
he gives no verdict on hearsay,
but judges the wretched with integrity,
and with equity gives a verdict for the poor of the land.
His word is a rod that strikes the ruthless,
his sentences bring death to the wicked.
Integrity is the loincloth round his waist,
faithfulness the belt about his hips.

The wolf lives with the lamb,
the panther lies down with the kid,
calf and lion cub feed together
with a little boy to lead them.
The cow and the bear make friends,
their young lie down together.
The lion eats straw like the ox.
The infant plays over the cobra's hole;
into the viper's lair
the young child puts his hand.
They do no hurt, no harm,
on all my holy mountain,
for the country is filled with the knowledge of the Lord
as the waters swell the sea.

That day, the root of Jesse
shall stand as a signal to the peoples.

28

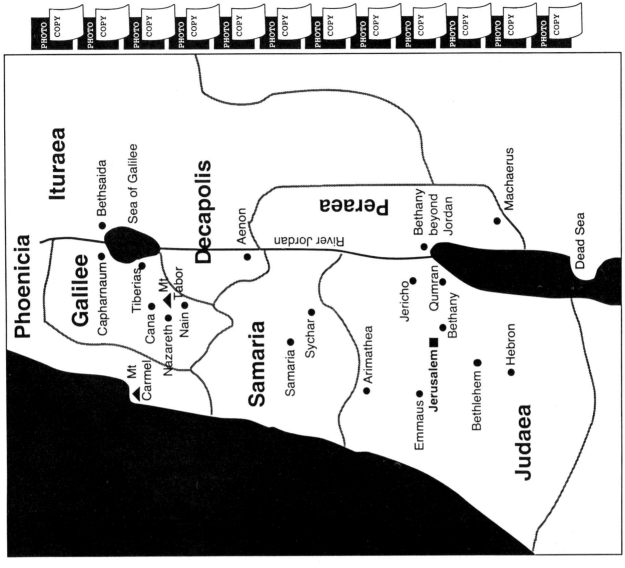

Gospel Reading: Matthew 1:13-25

Jesus is born of Mary who was betrothed to Joseph, son of David.

This is how Jesus Christ came to be born. His mother Mary was betrothed to Joseph; but before they came to live together she was found to be with child through the Holy Spirit. Her husband Joseph, being a man of honour and wanting to spare her publicity, decided to divorce her informally. He had made up his mind to do this when the angel of the Lord appeared to him in a dream and said, 'Joseph, son of David, do not be afraid to take Mary home as your wife, because she has conceived what is in her by the Holy Spirit. She will give birth to a son and you must name him Jesus, because he is the one who is to save his people from their sins'. Now all this took place to fulfil the words spoken by the Lord through the prophet: The virgin will conceive and give birth to a son and they will call him Emmanuel, a name which means 'God-is-with-us'. When Joseph woke up he did what the angel of the Lord had told him to do: he took his wife to his home.

29

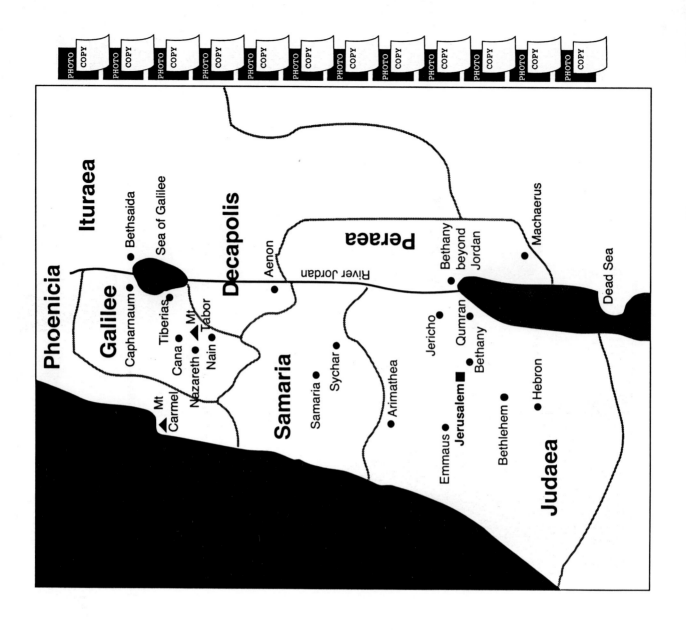

Old Testament Reading: Isaiah 35:1-6. 10

God himself is coming to save you.

Let the wilderness and the dry-lands exult,
let the wasteland rejoice and bloom,
let it bring forth flowers like the jonquil,
let it rejoice and sing for joy.

The glory of Lebanon is bestowed on it,
the splendour of Carmel and Sharon;
they shall see the glory of the Lord,
the splendour of our God.

Strengthen all weary hands,
steady all trembling knees
and say to all faint hearts,
Courage! Do not be afraid.

'Look, your God is coming,
vengeance is coming,
the retribution of God;
he is coming to save you.'

Then the eyes of the blind shall be opened,
the ears of the deaf unsealed,
then the lame shall leap like a deer
and the tongues of the dumb sing for joy;
for those the Lord has ransomed shall return.

They will come to Zion shouting for joy,
everlasting joy on their faces;
joy and gladness will go with them
and sorrow and lament be ended.

30

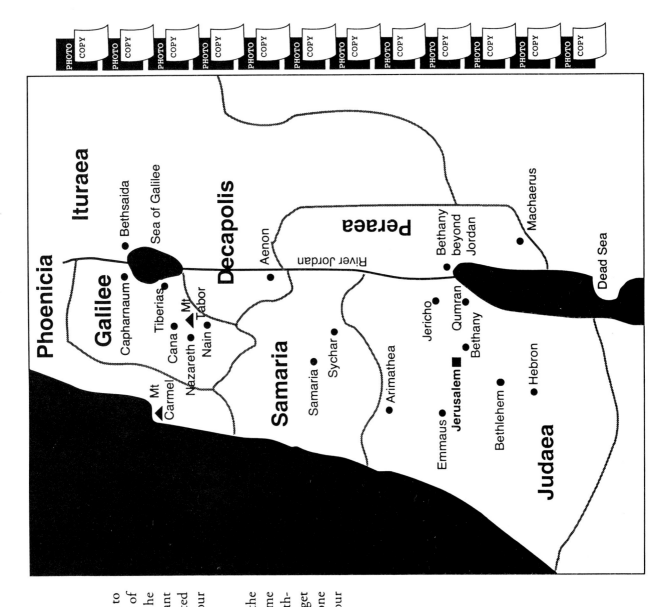

New Testament Reading: Romans 15:4-9

Christ is the saviour of all men.

Everything that was written long ago in the scriptures was meant to teach us something about hope from the examples scripture gives of how people who did not give up were helped by God. And may he who helps us when we refuse to give up, help you all to be tolerant with each other, following the example of Christ Jesus, so that united in mind and voice you may give glory to the God and Father of our Lord Jesus Christ.

It can only be to God's glory, then, for you to treat each other in the same friendly way as Christ treated you. The reason Christ became the servant of circumcised Jews was not only so that God could faithfully carry out the promises made to the patriarchs, it was also to get the pagans to give glory to God for his mercy, as scripture says in one place: For this I shall praise you among the pagans and sing to your name.

31

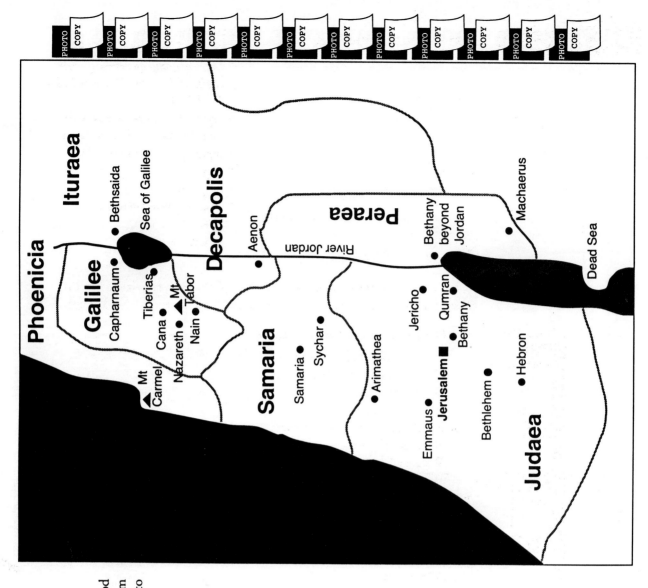

Old Testament Reading: Isaiah 7:10-14

The maiden is with child.

Once again the Lord spoke to Ahaz and said, 'Ask the Lord your God for a sign for yourself coming either from the depths of Sheol or from the heights above.' 'No', Ahaz answered, 'I will not put the Lord to the test.'

Then he said:

'Listen now, House of David:
are you not satisfied with trying the patience of men
without trying the patience of my God, too?
The Lord himself, therefore,
will give you a sign.
It is this: the maiden is with child
and will soon give birth to a son
whom she will call Immanuel,
a name which means "God-is-with-us" '.

Behind our masks

Things you will need
- *copies of opening prayer (p.33)*
- *copies of group questions (p.34)*
- *copies of the poem, 'Don't be fooled' (pp.34-5)*
- *copies of the scripture texts referred to on p.35; one text for each pupil*
- *copies of the prayers on p.38*
- *crayons*
- *art paper*
- *copies of prayers of teenagers*
- *reflective music*
- *a large candle*

Opening Prayer

Light the candle in the centre of the room. Play reflective music in the background. Distribute copies of the opening prayer to each pupil.

Handout

PHOTO COPY
PHOTO COPY
PHOTO COPY
PHOTO COPY
PHOTO COPY
PHOTO COPY
PHOTO COPY

This prayer was written by a teenager:

Sometimes I wonder who I am
and what it means to be me.
I look in the mirror
and see my reflection,
but all I get is another question.
'Who am I?'
'Who made me?'
'Who created this world of ours?'

As I look up into the sky,
looking for the answers to my thoughts,
a powerful sensation hits my face
and fills me with warmth and compassion.
At first I say
it's just the sun,
but then I realise
it's the answers to my questions.

The one who created the sun and the sky
and filled my heart with love and compassion
is the same one who let me be
and placed me in this world.
God is the answer to all my questions
and fills my mind with thoughts.
God is truly the light of the world,
the light that fills my heart.
Anne Frank

Read each question slowly, allowing a moment for reflection.
1. Do you sometimes wonder who you are and what it means to be you?
2. Do you ever look in the mirror and ask 'Who am I?'

Story
Another teenager
This is what Anne Frank wrote in her internationally famous *Diary:*

'...let me put it more clearly since no one will believe that a girl of thirteen feels herself quite alone in the world, nor is it so. I have darling parents and a sister of sixteen.

I know about thirty people whom one might call friends. I have strings of boyfriends, anxious to catch a glimpse of me and who, failing that, peep at me through mirrors in class. I have relations, aunts and uncles who are darling too, a good home, no – I don't seem to lack anything. But it's the same with all my friends, just fun and joking, nothing more. I can never bring myself to talk of anything outside the common round. We don't seem to be able to get any closer, that is the root of the trouble. Perhaps I lack confidence, but anyway, there it is, a stubborn fact that I don't seem to be able to do anything about.'

Handout

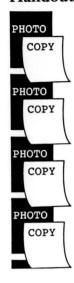

In groups of three or four discuss the following questions:

1. If you were to choose one word to describe how Anne is feeling what would it be? Give reasons for your choice.

2. Is the relationship she has with her friends – 'just fun and joking, nothing more' – the kind of relationship most teenagers have with their friends?

3. Anne says 'I could never bring myself to talk of anything outside the common round'. Why do you think this is so?

4. What kind of relationship do you think Anne would like to have with her friends?
    Would this be true of other teenagers?

5. Can you think of any IMAGE that would describe all of this?

    - *Distribute copies of these questions to each group.*
    - *Allow sufficient time for discussion.*
    - *One pupil in each group will feed back the points they have come up with.*
    - *Record a summary of the points on the blackboard, especially No. 5 – images.*

Masks

One image that could be used here is MASKS.
We will listen carefully to the following extract and see how much it could be our personal poem.

Poem

Read this poem with music playing in the background.

Handout

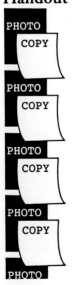

Don't be Fooled

Don't be fooled by me.
Don't be fooled by the face I wear
For I wear a thousand masks,
masks that I am afraid to take off,
and none of them are me.

I give the impression that I'm secure
that all is sunny and unruffled with me,
within as well as without,
that confidence is my name…
that the water's calm and I'm in command
and that I need no one.
But don't believe me please.
My surface may seem smooth
but my surface is my mask…

34

Behind this lies the real me in confusion,
in fear and aloneness.
But I hide this. I don't want anyone to know,
I panic at the thought of my weakness
and fear of being exposed.
That's why I frantically create a mask to hide behind,
…to help me pretend,
to shield me from the glance that knows.
But such a glance is precisely my salvation.
My only salvation. And I know it.
That is if it's followed by acceptance,
if it's followed by Love.
It's the only thing that will assure me
of what I cannot assure myself,
that I am worth something.

Only you can call me into aliveness.
Each time you're kind and gentle and encouraging
each time you try to understand
because you really care.
My heart begins to grow wings, very small wings,
very feeble wings, but wings…

You alone can break down the wall
behind which I tremble,
You alone can remove my mask
You alone can release me
from my shadow world of panic and uncertainty.

Do not pass me by.
Please, do not pass me by…

We all wear masks and, for various reasons, hide our true selves.
- Think for a moment of the masks you wear:
  – hiding what?
  – from whom?
  – why?

- Now, choose one of your masks, the one you think you wear most often.
  Write a letter to or a dialogue with this mask, e.g.
  Me: Today I wore you when…
  Mask: Why?

  Allow sufficient time for this exercise.
  Then ask the pupils to put it aside for the moment.

Scripture
Other people who wore masks:

1. John 8: 1-11: the adulterous woman
2. Luke 7: 36-50: the woman with a bad name
3. Mark 10: 17-23: The rich young man
4. Luke 19: 1-10: Zacchaeus

*Photocopy these texts from your bible and distribute a copy of ONE text to each pupil.
Allow personal time for the pupils to work on the following and answer the questions.*

- Read the text a number of times.
- Underline words and phrases that you think are significant.
- Who is the person wearing the mask in this story?
- Why is he or she wearing a mask?
- Does anybody see beyond the mask?
- What do you think is the result?
- Is there any connection between this Gospel text and the poem 'Don't be fooled'?
- What is the Gospel extract saying to you personally?

Reflection

Entrusting the mask to Jesus

- *The pupils take time to talk to the Lord about the way he saw behind people's masks. Invite them to ask him quietly to see behind theirs.*
- *Ask the pupils to come forward one at a time and place the 'letter' or 'dialogue' with their predominant mask around the large central candle. Then ask them to light a small candle from the main one.*
- *When all are seated once again ask them to think about the times when they didn't want to see behind the 'needy' masks of family and friends.*
  Provide a quiet moment here to ask God's forgiveness now that we can see the light (of the candle).
- *Ask each pupil, in turn, to bring his or her small candle and place it around the large candle and on top of the 'letters' and 'dialogues' that have already been placed there.*
  When all the pupils have done this invite them to pray for a moment for eyes to see behind the needy masks of other people.
- *Invite them to ask God, in the quiet of their hearts, that other people would have eyes to see behind the pupils' 'needy' masks also.*

Guided meditation

Close your eyes or focus on the candle.
Become aware of your breathing – the steady rhythm in and out, in and out.
Feel yourself relax.
Sense the stillness of the room.

In your imagination go to a quiet place – a room where you like to be, alone with just your own thoughts and feelings. Quietly recall the last time you were in this quiet room. You needed to be alone, by yourself. What were your thoughts and your feelings on that occasion?

As you spend time in this quiet place you become aware that there is a large chest in the corner of the room. It looks familiar yet you know that most times you hardly notice it. Slowly, you make your way to the chest and you open it. Inside you find several masks – a whole variety of sizes, shapes and colours. You notice that some look as though they have been used more than others.

You pick up one of the most used masks and you realise it is the mask you wear when…. How used it looks! Slowly you pick up some of the other masks one by one, thinking of when and why you wear each mask.
Be aware of your thoughts and your feelings.

You then sit down beside the chest, grateful that you have noticed it, grateful also that you have made friends with the masks that were inside it. As you sit there, relaxed, you begin to wonder if there is anyone at all who sees behind the masks you wear.

Then, slowly but clearly, you hear the following words as though you yourself were saying them:

> O, God, you search me and you know me.
> You know all about me: when I'm resting and when I'm working.
> You have probed my deepest intentions, tracking out the road I take…
> You know me through and through, understanding better than I
> what I'm trying to say.
> You have put your hand on my shoulder – why?
> All this is beyond me, out of my reach – I can't grasp it.
> Where can I go to escape you?
> You are wherever I am.
> If I climb the skies or explore the underworld, you are there!
> If I fly with the sun from dawn to dark, your hand is still on my shoulder, your
> right hand grips me!
> If I say 'I'll lose myself in the darkness, vanish in the night!' darkness is no dark-
> ness to you, night is as bright as day, darkness is light.
> I thank you for being what you are – awe-inspiring, wonderful,
> wonderful in all you do.
> You have made me the person I am in the depth of my being;
> you have known what I am really like from the moment I was born.
> You have watched the marvel of my body,
> the wonder of my birth:
> You've seen me grow up and marked all I've done –
> No day passed by uncounted, slipped by unnoticed.
> What you think of me matters to me, O God, more than anything else.…

As you listen to these words be aware of your feelings.

As the words end you remain seated by the chest for some time, aware that you are not alone, but that God is there beside you. God, too, has opened the chest and seen the masks, and you know there is no need to hide from God. You relax, knowing that God loves you.

It is time for you to leave this quiet room with the chest of masks. But God who knows and understands and loves you is there.

Once more become aware of your breathing in and out.

When you are ready open your eyes.

Illustrate whatever was important to you during this meditation.

Share with the class group a word or reflection on what they illustrated from the meditation.

My prayer
We began today by quoting a prayer written by a teenager. Now we will take a look at two more prayers, also written by teenagers.

Give each pupil a copy of these prayers:

Handout

I have locked myself in my own world, God. The door is locked. There is no key. It is very lonely, God. It is very dark and very cold. People knock, God. They want to come in. How can I let them?

Many times in our life we feel lonely. Often enough we feel abandoned by others, we feel drowned in our sorrows and that no one cares about or loves us. Our family loves us. God loves us. For all those times that we have felt lonely and locked ourselves behind doors, afraid of letting people in, may we always be able to turn to God, for it is he who can unlock the door.
Dreams Alive

Dear God,
I want to thank you, most of all for being a good listener.
Even when I don't ask you to hear my words, you are always there, and you pay attention anyways.
No matter how much I have to say or how long I chatter on, you are always very patient, you never interrupt or contradict me, and I know that I can trust you with my biggest secrets.
Thank you for listening to me cry for days and days when my first 'love' didn't work out, and thank you for being patient when I prayed for a million different things for my birthday.
Thank you for not telling Mom and Dad all the awful things that I say about them when I get angry, and also thank you for just being silent and giving me the opportunity to let my feelings out.
You are never judgemental about anything I say, and I don't need to hide anything from you.
You speak no words, yet I know you listen, not just with your mind, but with your heart.
Without fail, you are always there when I need you.
When I call, I never get the answering machine or the busy signal, any time of night.
You're never too tired to take the time to hear me speak.
Thank you, God, for your attentive ear and for always finding my words important enough to listen to.
Dreams Alive

Ask the pupils:
- What came to your mind as you read the first prayer?
  How is it similar to the image of MASKS which we have been sharing on today?
- What are the similarities between the second prayer and the meditation we had?
- Write your own prayer to God.

Allow the pupils a quiet time with reflective music in background to:
- *pray their own prayer*
  and/or
- *share their prayer with the class*

Seasonal colours/our world

Things you will need
- *a scarf to act as blindfold*
- *a tape of reflective music*
- *strips of coloured material (optional)*
- *crayons*
- *art paper*
- *a large candle*
- *a tape of music for dance*
- *copies of reflection guide-lines for each pupil (p.42)*
- *copies of 'Primrose' (p.42), by Patrick Kavanagh, one for each pupil*

Introduction

- This is a very busy time for each of us with study, other school activities and our life outside of school. So, as we come to this space in our day-to-day lives, let us try to relax our bodies and our minds.
- Let us take a minute or two to look back over the past week – the moments that were pleasant, and, perhaps, the moments that were difficult or unpleasant. For the next few hours let us try gently to put the happenings of the week aside and become present to the moment that is now.
- We have Jesus present with us, as represented by our lighted candle, so perhaps we could, in our hearts, lay our week before him.
- Quiet.

Setting the scene

A day like this when it is cold and the sky is overcast is the kind of time when people would like to relax at the fireside and tell stories. This is precisely what people did before TV made inroads into our homes. They say the Irish were particularly good as story-tellers – something to do with the Celtic imagination.

So, let's pretend. We are sitting by the fire and today the lot falls to me to tell the first story. As our story will shortly unfold I would ask you to try to forget that you have ever heard it so that you can enter into it in a way you have never done before.

Firstly, however, have you ever wondered what it must be like to be blind? Perhaps you played 'blind man's buff' as a child. Can you recall it and what it felt like?

Or, later on, perhaps, you did a trust walk when someone blindfolded you and then led you around?

Today, instead of being an onlooker in the Gospel story, really get into a blind person's shoes and try to live the story.

Mime/role play

To help us to do this I need two volunteers. *These go outside the door.*
They come into the room – one blindfolded, the other leading her.
I want us all to imagine that we are X, the blind person.

As you enter the room you take on the state of being blind. You leave behind memories of having been able to see. Slowly and gently allow these memories to leave you and just be present to darkness.
X is led gently around the room. At times, allow X to stand alone.
And all the time there is darkness.
And all the time we try to feel ourselves into X's place.
Ask X to share with the group what it was like to experience this darkness.
Does anyone else want to do the mime?

Sharing

Ask the others in the group what it was like to take part in this role play.

Scripture

Now, with some insight into what it is like to be blind, let us close our eyes once again and listen to a story.

Come in touch with your breathing – in and out – and relax in the steadiness of the life that is flowing through you. Become aware of the quiet in the room.

As Jesus was leaving Jericho with his disciples and a great multitude, Bartimaeus, a blind beggar, was sitting by the roadside. And when he heard that it was Jesus of Nazareth, he began to cry out and say, 'Jesus, Son of David, have mercy on me!' And many rebuked him, telling him to be silent; but he cried out all the more, 'Son of David, have mercy on me!' And Jesus stopped and said, 'Call him'. And they called the blind man, saying to him, 'Take heart; rise, he is calling you'. And throwing off his mantle he sprang up and came to Jesus. And Jesus said to him 'What do you want me to do for you?' And the blind man said to him, 'Master, let me receive my sight'. And Jesus said to him, 'Go your way; your faith has made you well'. And immediately he received his sight and followed him on the way'. *(Mk 11:46-52)*

Guided reflection

Can you recall times when you were blind – blind to God's presence in your own life or in the lives of others?

Perhaps for these times you would like to say, as Bartimaeus did, 'Jesus, son of David, have mercy on me'.

For a moment I would like you to stay with the question that Jesus asks each one of us: 'What do you want me to do for you?' Talk to Jesus about what you want of him. *Pause*

Perhaps each one of us is asking in some way for light, for sight ... to see meaning in our lives, to see what direction our lives might take, to see where our relationships are at, to see. *Pause*

And our scripture story tells us 'And immediately he received his sight'.

At this point, having received new sight, we are ready to move into our second story.

Our world

Read slowly:

Close your eyes and feel the stillness. Relax and become part of the quiet ... peacefully, silently.

Imagine that you have never seen creation, the world around you, never seen shape or colour ... that all is darkness.

Then imagine that into this darkness God steps out on space and he looks around and says
'I'm lonely – I'll make me a world'.

As far as the eye can see darkness covers everything
Blacker than a hundred midnights.

Then God smiles ... and the light breaks.
The darkness rolls up on one side ...
And the light stands shining on the other.
And God says 'That's good'.

Then God reaches out and takes the light in his hands
And God rolls the light around in his hands....
Until he makes the sun;
And he sets the sun ablazing in the heavens.

And the light that is left from making the sun God gathers up into a shining ball ...
And flings it against the darkness ....
Spangling the night with the moon and stars.

Then down between the darkness and the light he hurls the world
And God says 'That's good'.

The sun rises that very first day – its gentle colours scattering the black darkness.

The darkness seems reluctant to leave but steadily the once warm and then pale shades of daybreak spread their arms wide over the darkness and dispel it.

Blue appears – masses of blue sea – and above it the blue sky smiles happily down in its nakedness.

Land appears – green – rich green stretches of land sweeping at times majestically skywards in mountainous peaks.

There are valleys nestling in the folds of the mountains and hills. ....Valleys and plains alive with a myriad flowers and trees – red and orange and mauve, yellow and green and brown ... And fruit trees adding their own delightful original colours to the scene.

A rainbow appears in the sky ..... the rainbow of colourful promise.

Then God walks around.
God looks around on all that he has made.
He looks at the sun.
And he looks at the moon.
He looks at the little stars.
And he looks at the world – his flowers and trees and fruit-filled world....
with its celebration of colour....

And God says 'That's good'.

In the quiet at the end of this guided meditation put coloured materials around the central candle.

Focus
Our blindness has been healed and we can see. We are now awake to colour. (*Indicate coloured material.*)

Colouring
I invite you, now that we are all aware of colours, to celebrate colour in whatever image comes to you, using the crayons provided.

Quiet time
Play s*oft music ... sea and bird music if possible. Allow 10-15 minutes or whatever seems appropriate.*

Sharing
Perhaps you would like to share whatever is appropriate for you from what you have created. As you do so please place your illustration near the central candle.

Dance (Optional)
Ask each pupil to come and take a piece of coloured material of their choice from near the candle. The dance is one of sending out blessing to the north, south, east and west of our world.

Time alone
Distribute Reflection Guidelines (p.42), to be used by the pupils if they wish to do so.
They may prefer just to reflect or pray quietly during this time. Allow 15 or 20 minutes or whatever seems appropriate.

During this time you may think of a sentence from scripture, a poem, a reflection of your own, an image that you might like to colour.... or whatever is meaningful for you. Or you may just want to stay quietly with the Lord.

Handout

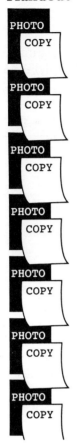

Reflection guidelines

1. Can I recall moments when God communicated with me through creation?
   - What helped me to see and hear?
   - What did God communicate?

2. What causes my 'blindness' – my lack of seeing and hearing on other occasions?
   - Are there similarities between the Gospel story of Bartimaeus and my story?

3. **Hymn**
   Most High, all-powerful, good Lord,
   Yours are the praises, the glory, the honour, and all blessing.
   To You alone, Most High, do they belong,
   and no man is worthy to mention Your name.
   Praised be You, my Lord, with all your creatures,
   especially Sir Brother Sun,
   Who is the day and through whom You give us light.
   And he is beautiful and radiant with great splendour;
   and bears a likeness of You, Most High One.
   Praised be You, my Lord, through Sister Moon and the stars,
   in heaven You formed them clear and precious and beautiful.
   Francis of Assisi, 'The Canticle of Brother Sun'

   - What is this saying to me?

4. Some people look at a leafless tree in winter and see something naked, without fruit, dead. Others look at it and are in touch with the life buried deep within it, its potential for new life, growth and fruitfulness.
   - Can I see ways in which the seasons reflect something of what is going on in my life?

Sharing

Ask the entire group to share on a word, a passage of scripture, a poem, an image ... whatever came to them during the meditation and/or quiet time.

Concluding song

'Song of Creation' (Monica Browne, *Celebrating our Journey*) *Play it quietly.*

Handout

Poem

Distribute this poem to the pupils.

Primrose

Upon a bank I sat, a child made seer
Of one small primrose flowering in my mind.
Better than wealth it is, said I, to find
One small page of Truth's manuscript made clear.
I looked at Christ transfigured without fear –
The light was very beautiful and kind,
And where the Holy Ghost in flame had signed
I read it through the lenses of a tear.
And then my sight grew dim, I could not see
The primrose that had lighted me to Heaven,
And there was but the shadow of a tree
Ghostly among the stars. The years that pass
Like tired soldiers nevermore have given
Moments to see wonders in the grass.

Patrick Kavanagh

Every common bush afire with God

Things you will need
- *a tape of song 'Speak Lord, I am Listening' (Monica Browne, Remembering Heart)*
- *copies of scripture reading on Moses (p.44)*
- *copies of adaptation of Genesis 28 (p.44)*
- *a tape of reflective music*
- *music for dance (optional)*
- *crayons*
- *art paper*
- *clay (optional)*
- *copies of song 'I will be with you' (p.47) (if not known already)*

Introduction

Stand at the crossroads and look,
ask for the ancient paths,
where the good way lies; and walk in it,
and find rest for your souls. *(Jr 6:16)*

- When you think that you are at a crossroads at this point of your life what words come spontaneously to your mind? *(Record on flip-chart/blackboard.)*
- It is a time in your life when the future very definitely reaches out to you, when you have dreams of what you would like that future to be. Yet, for anybody at a crossroads it is important to look back as well as forward, maybe also to look beyond as well as to look at. Perhaps we all look for the magical city of our dreams like the man in this rabbinical story.

Story

The City of Dreams

In the hiddenness of time there was a poor man who left his village, weary of his life, longing for a place where he could escape all the struggles of this earth. He set out in search of a magical city – the heavenly city of his dreams, where all things would be perfect. He walked all day and by dusk found himself in a forest, where he decided to spend the night. Eating the crust of bread he had brought, he said his prayers and, just before going to sleep, placed his shoes in the centre of the path, pointing them in the direction he would continue the next morning. Little did he imagine that while he slept, a practical joker would come along and turn his shoes around, pointing them back in the direction from which he had come.

The next morning, in all the innocence of folly, he got up, gave thanks to the Lord of the Universe, and started on his way again in the direction that his shoes pointed. For a second time he walked all day, and toward evening finally saw the magical city in the distance. It wasn't as large as he had expected. As he got closer, it looked curiously familiar. But he pressed on, found a street much like his own, knocked on a familiar door, greeted the family he found there – and lived happily ever after in the magical city of his dreams.

What is the truth contained in this story?

- The world we live in is fast-moving, noisy and busy. It is also a world that is colourful, creative and beautiful. The challenge facing us is to have eyes to see beauty, creativity and colour even amidst the noise, the speed and the busyness. This challenge hopefully will lead each one of us to become aware of God in our everyday lives.... not waiting for the magical city but discovering God in the gift that is now.

43

- We ask God, then, to help us to listen as he speaks to us during the time we have set aside today to spend very specially in his presence.

Song

'Speak, Lord, I am listening' (Monica Brown, *Remembering Heart)*

Scripture

People in the Bible encounter God in their everyday experiences

For example, Moses' experience of meeting God in the wilderness:
- *Read this account from Exodus. Play reflective music in background.*

Handout

Now Moses was keeping the flock of his father-in-law, Jethro, the priest of Midian; he led his flock to the west side of the wilderness, and came to Horeb, the mountain of God. There the angel of the Lord appeared to him in a flame of fire out of a bush; and he looked and the bush was blazing, yet it was not consumed. And Moses said, 'I must turn aside and look at this great sight, and see why the bush is not burned up.' When the Lord saw that he turned aside to see, God called to him out of the bush, 'Moses! Moses!' And he said, 'Here I am'. Then he said, 'Come no closer! Remove the sandals from your feet, for the place on which you are standing is holy ground'. And he said, 'I am the God of your father, the God of Abraham, the God of Isaac, and the God of Jacob'. And Moses hid his face, for he was afraid to look at God. *(Ex 3:1-6)*

- *Encourage reflective reading of this passage.*
  Distribute copies of reading.
  Ask the pupils to underline words and phrases which strike them.
  What do these words or phrases say to them?

Sharing

Share on these without comment.

- We have several Old and New Testament examples of people experiencing their 'now' as a meeting with God.
- *Distribute copies of this account from Genesis 28.*

Handout

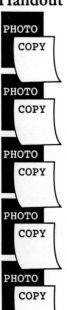

Jacob took a stone for a pillow,
put it under his head, and went to sleep.
As he dreamed, God told him,
'Know that I am here with you
In this place
and wherever you will go.
I will not leave you.'
Jacob awoke from his sleep and said,
'How amazing this place is!
This is nothing less than the house of God;
this is the gate of heaven!'
Rising early in the morning,
Jacob took the stone he had used for his pillow,
and set it up as a monument.
(Adapted from Genesis 28:15-18)
Earthsongs

- The NRSV translation of this gives the experience very beautifully (vv. 16 and 17): 'Surely the Lord is in this place – and I did not know it....
  How awesome is this place.....'
- In Luke 24:31 we hear that the two disciples who shared a simple meal with Jesus in Emmaus experienced their eyes being opened and recognising him

Reflection

An Invitation
Come to a quiet place,
a place so quiet
that you can hear
the grass grow.
Run your fingers
through the softness
of its petals,
and listen:
listen to the earth,
the warm earth,
the life pulse
of us all.
Rest your body
against its warmth;
feel its greatness,
the pulse and throb,
the foundation
of the world.
Look up into the sky,
the all-embracing sky,
the canopy of heaven.
How small
we really are:
specks in the greatness
but still a part of it all.
We grow from the earth
and find
our own place.

Our own 'meeting God' experiences
An invitation: Go to a quiet place. Reflect on moments in your own past when you felt you were encountering God in a special way. Make a note of these.
Allow a quiet time for this.

Sharing

Share in twos or threes, or in whatever grouping is comfortable with the particular class.

Dance (Optional)

We return to Moses' encounter with God and read there that God said to him 'Take off your shoes because the place where you stand is holy ground'.
This is an invitation to honour, reverence, respect these special 'meeting God' moments. Perhaps we could do this by dancing the Menusis – a reflective circular movement. As we get into the rhythm let us imagine that we circle these 'holy places' that we have experienced. Let us hold them with reverence, and let us give thanks.

45

Reflection

The 'everydayness' of 'holy places'

The poet Elizabeth Barrett Browning wrote:

> Earth's crammed with heaven
> And every common bush afire with God;
> But only he who sees takes off his shoes
> The rest sit round and pluck blackberries.

Let us, for a moment, get in touch with the reasons within ourselves that prevent us from seeing 'every common bush afire with God', and let us ask God to help us to see. Let us ask him, also, that we may respect what we see.

Take a few quiet moments to reflect that the way we experience ourselves standing on holy ground is in relationship.

> The world and all that is in it belong to Yahweh,
> the earth and all who live on it.
> Yahweh built it on the deep waters,
> laid its foundations in the ocean's depths.
> Who has the right to climb Yahweh's mountain?
> Or stand in this holy place?
> Those who are pure in act and in thought,
> who do not worship idols
> or make false promise.
> *(Adapted from Psalm 24:1-4)*
> *Earthsongs*

Story

Meeting God in others

Time before time, when the world was young, two brothers shared a field and a mill, each night dividing evenly the grain they had ground together during the day. One brother lived alone; the other had a wife and a large family. Now the single brother thought to himself one day, 'It isn't really fair that we divide the grain evenly. I have only myself to care for, but my brother has children to feed.' So each night he secretly took some of his grain to his brother's granary to see that he was never without.

But the married brother said to himself one day, 'It isn't really fair that we divide the grain evenly, because I have children to provide for me in my old age, but my brother has no one. What will he do when he's old?' So every night he secretly took some of his grain to his brother's granary. As a result, both of them always found their supply of grain mysteriously replenished each morning.

Then one night they met each other halfway between their two houses, suddenly realised what had been happening, and embraced each other in love. The story is that God witnessed their meeting and proclaimed, 'This is a holy place – a place of love – and here it is that my temple shall be built.' And so it was. The holy place, where God is made known to people, is the place where human beings discover each other in love.

- Do you know of other situations like this from life, books, films?
- Have you ever experienced anything like the incident in this story?

Guided meditation

Close your eyes. Become aware of your breathing – your breathing in and out.... the gift of life and living.

Become aware of the stillness.

Allow your thoughts to journey back gently over the past few years... your time in second-level school. Visit once again the first days and weeks you spent here. Recall your thoughts and your feelings....

Revisit your time spent in this class group..... and the other important aspects of being part of this school.

Travel, slowly, along the road of this year, spending time with moments that were special for you..... moments when you felt that God was with you. Stay with these moments as they begin to surface again now in your heart and mind.

Focus on the moment itself.... the significant people of that moment.... the God who was with you at that moment. Be aware of your thoughts and feelings as you move along through the year....

Perhaps there will be times during this gentle journey when you will hear God call you by name as he called Moses in the wilderness...

You listen and you respond......

You continue to journey through the year..... at times pausing to take off your shoes..... to tune into the specialness of the moment.... and to give thanks.....

As you journey back to the present moment allow an image to come to you.... an image of the past months or an image of one particular moment that was special for you. Stay with that image.... hold it with respect..... Spend some time talking to God about this image.

When you are ready open your eyes.

Colouring

- Spend some time quietly responding to the meditation.
- Illustrate your image in colour or clay.

Sharing

- Light a large candle in the centre of the room.
- Each pupil will share whatever is appropriate about her or his image and then place it near the candle.

We have been reflecting on the times when we experienced God's presence in our everyday lives. Whatever our feelings about the future, he assures us of one thing:

Handout

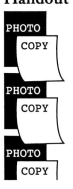

Song

'I will be with you' (*Songs of the Spirit*, 45)

> I will be with you wherever you go
> Go now throughout the world
> I will be with you in all that you say
> Go now and spread my word.
>
> Come, walk with me on stormy waters
> Why fear? Reach out and I'll be there.

From darkness to sunshine

Things you will need
- *newspaper cuttings on the theme of 'death'*
- *reflective music*
- *copies of questions for reflection (p.49)*
- *a large candle*
- *a tape of 'Life', (Monica Browne,* God of my Life*)*
- *a tape of music for dance (optional)*
- *small candles — one for each pupil*

Begin with Taizé chants around the cross, e.g. 'Stay here and keep watch with me'.

Introduction

Death

Every day in the media we hear of death:

- accidents
- murders
- natural causes
- earthquakes, flooding, etc.

What words or images come to you when you hear the word 'death'?

What is it like for people when someone they love dies?

How do you think they feel as they think of the future without this person?

What do you think is the greatest need of a person who has just seen someone they love die?

Read:

'Standing near the cross of Jesus were his mother and his mother's sister, Mary the wife of Clopas, and Mary Magdalene' (*Jn 19:25*).

Let us imagine that we too are standing here at the foot of the cross watching Jesus die. What are your thoughts, what are your feelings as you stand there with Mary and the others?

Allow a quiet time for this with soft music in the background.

Read:

'Now there was a garden in the place where he was crucified and in the garden there was a new tomb in which no one had ever been laid. So, because it was the Jewish day of Preparation, and the tomb was nearby, they laid Jesus there' (*Jn 19:41-42*).

Guided meditation

Close your eyes or focus on the candle. Relax. Become aware of your breathing.

In your imagination go to this garden and find yourself outside the tomb where Jesus has been laid. You came here just to be quiet for a while.... to remember what it was like for you when Jesus was alive.....

What it is like for you now that he is dead....

Then you leave the tomb and you go to the building where you know the apostles and the other friends of Jesus are. They are in the room upstairs, the Upper Room. They look extremely frightened as you enter the room and you know that they are afraid that the Jews will punish them as they punished Jesus. You look around slowly at each of them. You go near to Peter and you hear him say: 'I denied him three times, said I never knew him. I ran away... didn't see him as he died. And he trusted me, trusted me...' Beside Peter is John, the disciple Jesus loved. John whispers in his deep sorrow: 'Well, I was there at the end. Is it the end? Is it the end... the end of all Jesus hoped for, lived for, died for? Is it the end?' Then Thomas says: 'Women! Mary Magdalene expecting us to believe that she saw Jesus alive again. Illusions – typical. I won't believe until I see – see his wounds'

You remember the cross and the dying Jesus..... you remember the tomb and the enormous sense of death. You listen to the apostles' grief, their questions. You sense the emptiness that Jesus' death has caused.

As you sit there thinking of Jesus' death, of the tomb where they laid him, of life without Jesus, you sense your energy leave you. What will life be like without Jesus? You feel surrounded by blackness.

Slowly, you sense a change in the very dismal atmosphere. The blackness you feel within and outside you begins to lighten – feel it lighten – and you sense a new energy in the air. You know that the others in this Upper Room feel the same excitement and – Jesus himself stands there. Stay with your thoughts and your feelings as you see Jesus – a Jesus who is alive. Then Jesus says: 'Peace be with you'.
Peace – Jesus wants to give you the gift of peace. Open your mind and your heart – the areas of your life where you don't experience peace – open yourself to receive Jesus' gift of peace.

As you receive this gift of peace you spend some time thanking Jesus for this gift, for all his gifts to you.

As you stay there peacefully with Jesus you become aware that the awful blackness that you sensed everywhere has been lifted. You look up and you look out from the Upper Room and you see colour, so many colours, golden wheat and fruits of all kinds. In the distance lambs play joyfully in the fields. The oppressive air has vanished and instead you clearly hear the singing of the birds. And in your heart you know:
This is new life – Jesus isn't dead, he is risen.
He is here among us, with you and me. Alleluia!

Pause for quiet reflection.

Handout

Questions for reflection

1. What was it like for you to be in the Upper Room with the disciples listening as they recalled Jesus' death?
   What were your thoughts and your feelings?

2. Did you sense a change from darkness to sunshine?
   Does an image come to you of what that was like?

3. What are the areas of your life where you don't experience peace?
   How did you feel when you received Jesus' gift of peace?

4. What images come to you of 'death that gives way to new life'?

Now illustrate (using crayons) what this meditation said to you.

Light the large candle.

Jesus is with us!

Sharing

- Place the illustration of your image in front of you.
- Share with the others whatever you feel comfortable sharing.
- Place your image around the large candle.

Song and/or dance

1. *Play 'Life' (Monica Browne,* God of my life), *allowing the pupils to join in when they have a good idea of the song.*
   Does this song express some of your own thoughts and feelings?

2. When we experience something deep like joy we usually want to share it. Let's send this joy out to north, south, east and west. Dance with coloured ribbons.

Scripture

Emmaus Journey – Witness

The disciples experienced sunshine after darkness when Jesus appeared to them after his death. Jesus wanted them to share this sunshine with others and he said to them: 'Thus it is written, that the Messiah is to suffer and to rise from the dead on the third day and that repentance and forgiveness of sins is to be proclaimed in his name to all nations beginning from Jerusalem. You are witnesses of these things' *(Luke 24:44-48).*

Sharing

In pairs share on the following:
1. What is the gospel or Good News that Jesus tells us to preach?
2. How have people shared the Good News with me?
3. How can I share the Good News with others?

Each participant in the group, in her or his own time, comes and lights a small candle from the central one.
She or he says briefly how she or he is challenged to be a witness to Jesus who has risen.

Blessing

After Jesus appeared to the disciples we hear that 'lifting up his hands he blessed them'.
Close your eyes.
- Ask yourself, 'What blessing do I want from Jesus?'
- Ask him for this blessing.
- Allow yourself to experience Jesus blessing you.
- Turn to the person next to you. Rest your hand on his or her shoulder and quietly pray that Jesus will bless this person also.

Jesus' promise
'I am with you always to the end of time'.

Hymn
'I will be with you wherever you go'.
(*Songs of the Spirit*)

Gifts and talents

Things you will need
- *copies of 'The Gift', by Patrick Kavanagh (p.51)*
- *copies of questionnaire based on the story 'The Portrait' (p.52)*
- *tape of song 'See the birds of the air'*
- *reflective music*
- *crayons*
- *art paper*
- *clay (optional)*
- *copies of questionnaire 'Where am I?' (p.54)*
- *copies of extracts on the theme 'Against all the odds' (pp.54-55)*

When you hear the words 'gifts and talents' what other words do you associate with them? Record on the blackboard or flip-chart.

Perhaps one of the aspects we associate with being gifted and talented is perfection – something that outstanding people seem to have but certainly not ordinary people like us.

Poem

Handout

The Gift

One day I asked God to give
Me perfection so I'd live
Smooth and courteous, calmly wise
All the world's virtuous prize

So I should not always be
Getting into jeopardy,
Being savage, wild and proud
Fighting, arguing with the crowd;

Being poor, sick, depressed,
Everywhere an awful pest;
Being too right, being too wrong.
Being too weak, being too strong.

Being every hour fated
To say the things that make me hated;
Being a failure in the end –
God, perfection on me spend.

And God spoke out of Heaven
The only gift in My giving
Is yours – Life, Seek in hell
Death, perfect, wise, comfortable   *Patrick Kavanagh*

Distribute copies of the poem.

Reflect quietly for a moment on the following:

What does this poem say to me about the difference between the gifts people ask God for and the gifts God, in fact, gives them?
Does this say anything to you:
a.   about God?
b.   about gifts?
c.   about you?
Share your answers in the group.

The gifts others see in us

God has given us the gift of life. Sometimes we want other gifts, as described in Patrick Kavanagh's poem. We can be blind to the gifts that we possess... the gifts that other people can see more easily.

Story

The portrait

Sidney Smith was something of a celebrity in the town where he lived. One day he decided to commission a local artist to paint his portrait. The artist did a preliminary sketch and showed it to Sidney for his approval. It was a perfect likeness, but Sidney was outraged.

'This isn't what I wanted at all!' he said. 'You've made my face look too round. You'll have to do it again.'

The painter did another sketch, but still Sidney wasn't satisfied.

'My shoulders don't look broad enough,' he said.

'Do it again, but this time do something about the shoulders.'

The artist did another sketch with a thinner face and broader shoulders.

Sidney shook his head impatiently. 'It's still not right,' he said. 'I think the shape of the chin is wrong, and the eyes are too small. I don't like the nose either.'

The painter did sketch after sketch, until finally Sidney was happy.

'Good,' he said. 'At last I'm beginning to like myself.'

When he took the portrait home, he invited all his friends and relations to come and see it. Everybody burst out laughing.

'What a dreadful artist!' they said. 'That doesn't look a bit like you. How could he portray you like that? He hasn't captured any of your qualities – the kindness of your face, the twinkle in your eyes. We think you look much nicer as you really are.'

When they'd all gone, Sidney looked at the picture in shame and embarrassment. He wrapped it in brown paper and took it back to the artist.

'I've changed my mind,' he said. 'I'd like you to do the portrait again, but this time make it like the original sketch you showed me. I've decided that's the one I like best.'

Handout

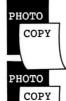

Distribute this questionnaire.

1. Why didn't Sidney like the first sketch?
2. What was Sidney really rejecting – the sketch or himself?
3. When Sidney said, 'At last I'm beginning to like myself,' was he being honest? When did he begin to like himself?
4. Why didn't his friends and family like the portrait?
5. What does this story tell us about our self-image?

   • Take time to answer these questions personally.
   • Share in threes or fours.
   • Feedback to class.

Song

'See the birds of the air' (Monica Brown, *Celebrating our Journey*)

If appropriate distribute copies of the words and ask the class to sing the song a number of times.

This song speaks of our image in God's eyes.

Guided meditation

Gifts

Close your eyes and rest your hands in a relaxed way on your lap. Listen to your breathing. As you relax more your breathing will become deeper. Perhaps your body is tired so relax and allow the tiredness to leave you. Then become aware of the quiet of the room.

In your imagination go to a favourite quiet place, a place where you like to go to be alone. As you sit in this favourite place allow the details of the scene to be filled in – the colours, the shapes, the sounds. Become aware, too, of your feelings in this favourite place.

As you are enjoying the peace and quiet you become aware of movement in the distance; coming slowly towards you is a person whom you gradually begin to recognise as some-one familiar. As he comes nearer you know that it is Jesus. You know too that he is pleased to see you here in your favourite place. When he reaches you he smiles at you in such a way that you know you are loved and then he sits down beside you.

Stay in Jesus' presence, aware of your thoughts and feelings.

Then he gives you his full attention and says: 'It's a long time now since you received your gifts. I would like us to talk about them'. You feel surprised, puzzled in fact. 'Gifts? What gifts, Jesus?'

'All those gifts that come to you with the great gift of life... you know, the gifts that make you different from everyone else'.

Then he slowly leads you through a precious time to rediscover those gifts. He says: 'Your gift of personality'. And then you see those beautiful qualities that others occa-sionally tell you that you have. Stay with them for a while.

Jesus continues: 'And your talents, those gifts that help you to do certain things well. Please don't take them for granted. They are gifts'. And again you allow yourself to bring your talents before you, and for the first time you admire them and you claim them.

Once again Jesus speaks: 'Your dreams, those wonderful dreams you have for your life and the world. Come in touch with those dreams. They are yours, very specially yours. They can give you life and through them you can give others life. Love your dreams. Care for them. Above all be grateful for them. They are yours. Your dreams are an ex-pression of you. Stay with your dreams and what they tell you about yourself'.

Perhaps there are now other aspects of yourself that you would like quietly to take a new look at. These, too, are gifts.

You become aware, as you are taking a look at yourself, as if for the first time, that Jesus too is looking at you. Then he calls you by your name and he says.

'I have given you many gifts because I love you.....'

As you return from your favourite quiet place you spend some time thanking Jesus for his gifts to you.

Guided meditation

Illustrate in colour (or clay) whatever the meditation is saying to you.
Share whatever is appropriate, perhaps showing your illustration and saying a brief word to the class.

Scripture

Confronting a parable

Distribute the parable of the pounds: Luke 19:11-26.

As they were listening to this, he went on to tell a parable, because he was near Jerusalem, and because they supposed that the kingdom of God was to appear immedi-ately. So he said, 'A nobleman went to a distant country to get royal power for himself and then return. He summoned ten of his slaves, and gave them ten pounds and said to them, 'Do business with these until I come back.' But the citizens of his country hated him and sent a delegation after him, saying, 'We do not want this man to rule over us.'

When he returned, having received royal power, he ordered these slaves, to whom he had given the money, to be summoned so that he might find out what they had gained by trading. The first came forward and said, 'Lord, your pound has made ten more pounds.' He said to him, 'Well done, good slave! Because you have been trustworthy in a very small thing, take charge of ten cities.' Then the second came, saying, 'Lord, your pound has made five pounds.' He said to him, 'And you, rule over five cities.' Then the other came, saying, 'Lord, here is your pound. I wrapped it up in a piece of cloth, for I was afraid of you, because you are a harsh man; you take what you did not deposit, and reap what you did not sow.' He said to him, 'I will judge you by your own words, you wicked slave! You knew, did you, that I was a harsh man, taking what I did not deposit and reaping what I did not sow? Why then did you not put my money into the bank? Then when I returned, I could have collected it with interest.' He said to the bystanders, 'Take the pound from him and give it to the one who had ten pounds.' (And they said to him, 'Lord, he has ten pounds!') 'I tell you, to all those who have, more will be given; but from those who have nothing, even what they have will be taken away.'

Allow a quiet time to answer the following questionnaire. Play reflective music in the background.

Handout

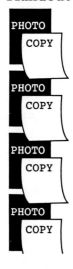

Where am I?

1. Name your gifts and talents. (Perhaps some of these came to mind during the meditation.)

2. Reflecting on the parable of the talents (or pounds), do you find yourself:
   a. developing 10?
   b. developing 5?
   c. putting your gift 'away safely'?

3. What are your thoughts and feelings about how you are:
   a. using
   b. developing
   c. not using
   your gifts?

4. What does this parable say to you?

5. What would you like to say to God about your gifts and talents?

If appropriate:
Some of you might like to share a thought on question 5. *Continue playing music in the background.*

Handout

Story

Against all the odds

I. JONI EARECKSON

In July 1967, when she was 17, Joni dived into a lake and broke her neck; since then she has been a quadriplegic, confined to life in a wheelchair. Joni has learned to paint with her mouth, and she writes books and gives lectures. Here is an extract from a letter to her from a friend, Steve, telling Joni how he sees her.

> So, Joni, when you're got to speak ten times in one week, when your jaw gets a little tired from smiling at well-wishers, when your back aches, when you've got a secret inner urge sometime to be on your feet but feel you can't express it cause the folks around you would take it wrong, when you miss your friends, when the Bible seems boring, when you feel insecure, when you find sinful thoughts and attitudes creeping into your head, when you're tempted to run mental

movies of your success and glory in yourself – in short ... when you feel like carrying a smooth cross and slipping a bit, even 'just for today' ... don't. Don't be discouraged, and don't sin. And don't feel the hassle is in vain, because you honestly have got to be one of the mainstays in my life when it comes to setting an example when I feel like quitting.

2. CHRISTOPHER NOLAN

Here is an extract from John Carey's preface to Christopher's second book, *Under the eye of the clock*.

For a preface which did not need writing in the first place, this has gone on long enough. But there is one thing to add. It would be possible to praise and analyse Nolan's book as one would the work of any brilliantly gifted young writer, without reference to his physical condition. That might, indeed, appear the tactful and seemly procedure. It would, however, be misguided in my opinion. The point is not that one has to make 'allowances'. Nolan's disability is not a handicap which has to be charitably offset against failures in accomplishment. Rather, it is a positive factor which adds immensely to the book's value and significance. For this is a voice coming from silence, and a silence that has, as Nolan is aware, lasted for centuries. He has a deep sense of the generations of mute, helpless cripples who have been 'dashed, branded and treated as dross', for want of a voice to tell us what it feels like. Now that voice – or at any rate that redeeming link with a typewriter – has come, and we know. On page after page of this book, Nolan tells us. It should not be possible, after reading it, ever again to think as we have before about those who suffer what he suffers. That is what makes it not just an outstanding book but a necessary one.

3. DAVOREN HANNA

Teenage Irish poet Davoren Hanna – who overcame massive disability to win a number of prestigious literary awards – died yesterday morning in a Dublin hospital.

The 19 year old writer, who had been ill for some time, died in St Mary's Hospital in Dublin's Phoenix Park after his condition deteriorated rapidly over the weekend.

His death came just four years after his mother, Brigid Woods Hanna, died of a heart attack, aged 44, while on a family holiday in Donegal.

Davoren was born with cerebral palsy and although he was diagnosed as mentally retarded, his mother spent hours reading to him and playing with plastic letters.

By the age of ten he had written over 300 poems and won first prize in junior poetry in the TSB Irish Schools Creative Writing competition. The Christy Brown Award, the British Spastics Society Literary Award and an award in The Observer National Children's Poetry Competition followed.

Davoren described his life without a means of expression in his book of poetry *Not Common Speech*. 'Can you imagine being trapped inside a burning building knowing the fire brigade couldn't hear your cries because the noise of breaking glass and crashing timber filled their ears? I inhaled the noxious fumes of platitudes, misunderstandings and misdiagnosis during my early years.'

With the help of a Department of Health carer, he attended Pobal Scoil Rosmini in Drumcondra where he sat his Leaving Cert last year.

Arrangements for his funeral tomorrow are being finalised. He is survived by his father, journalist Jack Hanna from Dublin's Drumcondra.
Irish Independent, 19 July 1994

What kind of people do you think Joni, Christopher and Davoren are?
What category would they fit into in the parable of the talents?
What are they saying to each of us?

Ask God to help you to be aware of and appreciate your talents.

55

Concluding prayer

Celebrate You!

You are worth celebrating.
You are worth everything.
You are unique.

In all the whole world,
there is only one you.
There is only one person
with your talents, your experience,
your gift.
NO ONE CAN TAKE YOUR PLACE!

God created only one you,
precious in his sight.
You have immense potential to love, to care,
to create,
to grow,
to sacrifice,
if you believe in yourself.

It doesn't matter your age, or your colour,
or whether your parents loved you or not.
(Maybe they wanted to but couldn't).
Let that go.
It belongs to the past.
You belong to the now.

It doesn't matter what you have been,
the wrong you've done,
the mistakes you've made,
the people you've hurt.
You are forgiven – you are accepted – you're OK.
You are loved in spite of everything.
So love yourself and nourish the good within you,
CELEBRATE YOU!

Begin now. Start afresh. Give yourself a new beginning. Today.
You are now, and that is all you need to be.
You cannot earn, or deserve, this new life.
It is given as a gift, freely.
That is the great miracle: that God loves you.
So celebrate the miracle and celebrate you! Be happy!

Challenged to grow

Things you will need
- *pictures of (a) a baby (b) a 9-or 10-year-old (c) a teenager*
  or
- *photographs of the pupils themselves at these stages*
- *copies of Patrick Kavanagh's poem 'From Failure Up', with questions based on it (pp.58-9)*
- *a tape of the song 'Listen, imagine' (Monica Browne,* Celebrating Our Journey)
- *reflective music*
- *copies of questions for personal reflection (p.60)*
- *crayons*
- *art paper*
- *clay (optional)*
- *seeds – at least one for each pupil*
- *a box with earth (in which to sow seeds)*

Story

The story of Jonathan Livingston Seagull is no ordinary story because Jonathan is no ordinary seagull. It is the story of someone who didn't hide behind limitations but reached out to growth.

Jonathan Livingston Seagull was no ordinary bird. Most gulls don't bother to learn more than the simplest facts of flight – how to get from shore to food and back again. For most gulls, it is not flying that matters but eating. For this gull, though, it was not eating that mattered but flight. More than anything else, Jonathan Livingston loved to fly.

This kind of thinking, he found, was not the way to make oneself popular with other birds. For the next few days he tried to behave like the other birds: he really tried, screeching and fighting with the flocks around the piers and fishing boats, diving on scraps of fish and bread. But he couldn't make it work. It's all so pointless, he thought. I could be spending all this time learning to fly. There's so much to learn! It wasn't long before Jonathan was off by himself again, far out at sea, hungry, happy, learning. But victory was shortlived. From now on I must be content as I am, as a poor limited seagull. He vowed he would return to the flock. It would make everyone happy.

'I am done with the way I was, I am done with everything I learned. I am a seagull like every other seagull and I will fly like one'. Ah, and it was pretty good; just to stop thinking and fly peacefully through the dark, towards the lights about the beach. Then, in the dark, a hundred feet in the air, Jonathan Livingston Seagull blinked. His pain, his resolutions, vanished. 'Short wings. A falcon's short wings! That's the answer! What a fool I've been. All I need is a tiny little wing. All I need is to fold most of my wings and fly just on the tips alone. All I need is short wings'.

His vows of a moment before were forgotten, swept away in that great swift wind. Yet he felt guiltless, breaking the promises he had made himself. Such promises are only for the gulls that accept the ordinary. One who can touch excellence in his learning has no need of that kind of promise.

How much more there is now to living! Instead of our drab slogging forth and back to the fishing boats, there's a reason to life. We can lift ourselves out of ignorance; we can find ourselves as creatures of excellence and intelligence and skill. We can be free; we can learn to fly.

1. How did Jonathan's attitude differ from that of the other birds?

2. What was the struggle that Jonathan went through?

3. What did flying mean to Jonathan (freedom, learning, overcoming limitations)?

4. In what ways could this be a parable for us?

Sharing

Life-line

a. *Show pictures of:*
   – a baby
   – a 9-10-year-old
   – a teenager
   or

b. *Have the pupils bring in photographs of themselves at these stages.*

Place the pictures at a distance from each other

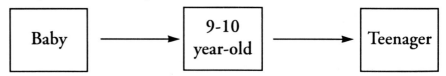

Ask the pupils to describe the stages of growth from babyhood to 10, and then from 10 to now.
Record these stages in the spaces between the pictures.

Draw your life-line:

_____

0   Along this life-line mark points of growth as you remember them.   16

Allow time for the pupils to reflect and mark in their points of growth.
- Name the area of growth
- What caused this growth?
- Were there significant people who helped this growth?
- Can you recall your thoughts and feelings about it?
- What was your picture of God at this time?

Share in small groups of three or four.

Poem

Distribute copies of this poem.

Handout

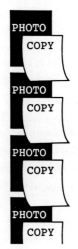

From Failure Up

Can a man grow from the dead clod of failure
Some consoling flower
Something humble as a dandelion or a daisy,
Something to wear as a buttonhole in Heaven?
Under the flat, flat grief of defeat maybe
Hope is a seed.
Maybe this is what he was born for, this hour
Of hopelessness.
Maybe it is here he must search
In this hell of unfaith
Where no one has a purpose
Where the web of meaning is broken threads

58

And one man looks at another in fear.
O God, can a man find You when he lies with his face downwards
And his nose in the rubble that was his achievement?
Is the music playing behind the door of despair?
O God, give us purpose.

Patrick Kavanagh

Ask the pupils to read the poem quietly, underlining the words that they think are significant.

Handout

Ask them:
- Why are these words significant?
- What is the tone of the poem?
- Is there any connection between this and *Jonathan Livingston Seagull?*
- Have you ever experienced anything of what Kavanagh is writing about?
- Can failure be a moment of growth? Why? Why not?
- Think back on the last time that you felt like Kavanagh. Did you learn anything from it?
- Failure is one experience through which we can grow. What are the other areas?

The potential for growth is reflected all around us. We have only to look at the cycle of nature in the seasons to see that dying and new life are part of the same reality.
There is a number of references to seeds in the Gospels.
One example is Matthew 13:31-32:

> He put before them another parable: 'The kingdom of heaven is like a mustard seed...; it is the smallest of all seeds, but when it has grown it is the greatest of shrubs and becomes a tree, so that the birds of the air come and make nests in its branches.'

Ask the pupils:
Could that seed be you?
Do you think that you are in touch with your potential for growth?

Song
'Listen, imagine' (Monica Browne, *Celebrating Our Journey*)

Guided meditation
Close your eyes or focus on the candle. In our meditation I would like you to try to listen to a parable as though you have never heard it before.
It is springtime and in your imagination you find yourself in the country walking leisurely through the fields. Feel the clear air and listen to the song of the birds. You sit down in one of the fields – a field that has been prepared for sowing. Jesus joins you there and sits beside you. Just be with Jesus on this morning in spring.
Soon he begins to tell you a story. He says: 'A sower went out to sow. And as he sowed some seeds fell along the path and the birds came and devoured them.' Then Jesus turns to you and says gently: 'I have wanted to sow seeds for growth in your life but sometimes you are like this stony path.'
You begin to reflect on the times when you have resisted growth. You talk to Jesus about these times and you tell him why you resist seeds of growth.
Jesus continues with his story: 'Other seeds fell on rocky ground where they had not much soil and immediately they sprang up, since they had no depth of soil, but when the sun rose they were scorched; and since they had no root they

withered away.' Slowly and gently, Jesus turns to you and asks: 'Are there times when the seed that I sow for your growth withers because you have no depth of soil? Think about these times.

And Jesus says: 'Other seeds fell upon thorns and the thorns grew up and choked them.' Jesus again asks gently – 'What are the obstacles in your life that make you like the thorn bushes?'

You spend some time quietly reflecting on those aspects in your life that are obstacles to growth.

Again you talk to Jesus about them.

Then Jesus continues: 'Other seeds fell on good soil and brought forth grain, some a hundredfold, some sixty and some thirty.' 'You have known these moments also', Jesus says to you, 'moments of growth, sometimes great growth'.

Be aware of your thoughts and your feelings as you hear Jesus say this to you.

You reflect on the areas of growth in your life and you give thanks.

You are gently becoming aware again of the clear spring air and the song of birds. You leave the field reflecting on what you have seen and you begin your journey back. When you are ready open your eyes.

Personal reflection

Distribute copies of these questions. Ask the pupils to answer them personally. Play music in the background.

Handout

1. In what ways am I like a seed?
2. In what ways am I like the soil?
   What qualities do I have which make me good soil?
3. The seed needs the right environment in which to grow. What in my environment (a) helps (b) hinders my growth?
4. All growth involves dying and new life.
   In what ways does this challenge me?
5. What are the areas in my life in which I would like to grow?
6. What image comes to me of 'the call to growth in my life'?

Answer these questions personally.

Illustrate the image using crayons or clay.

Place the photographs of the pupils in the centre of the room.
Each pupil should place an image next to these pictures.

Ask them to share a word, a sentence, a reflection – whatever is appropriate.

Ask each pupil to take a seed from a box near the images and sow it in a large box, quietly asking God to help him or her to become soil that will enable great growth.

Reread the parable of the mustard seed.

Concluding prayer

Called to become

You are called to become
A perfect creation.
No one is called to become
Who you are called to be.

It does not matter
How short or tall
Or thick-set or slow
You may be.
It does not matter
Whether you sparkle with life
Or are silent as a still pool,
Whether you sing your song aloud
Or weep alone in darkness.
It does not matter
Whether you feel loved and admired
Or unloved and alone
For you are called to become
A perfect creation.
No one's shadow
Should cloud your becoming,
No one's light
Should dispel your spark.
For the Lord delights in you,
Jealously looks upon you
And encourages with gentle joy
Every movement of the Spirit
Within you.
Unique and loved you stand,
Beautiful or stunted in your growth
But never without hope and life.
For you are called to become
A perfect creation.
This becoming may be
gentle or harsh,
Subtle or violent,
But it never ceases,
Never pauses or hesitates,
Only is –
Creative force –
Calling you
Calling you to become
A perfect creation.
From Psalms of a Laywoman, Edwina Gately

Resource list

Audio tapes

Celebrating Our Journey	Monica Browne
Remembering Heart	Monica Browne
God of My Life	Monica Browne
Glory and Praise	Oregon Catholic Press
Journey of the Robin	Seamus Byrne
Laudate	Taizé

(All available from Veritas, 7/8 Lower Abbey Street, Dublin 1. Tel 01-878 8177)

Peace	David Sun
Tranquillity	David Sun
Resonance	Terry Oatfield
Silver Wings	Mike Rowland
The Fairy Ring	Mike Rowland

(All available from Scripture Union, 40 Talbot Street, Dublin 1. Tel 01-836 3764)

Godspell	
When A Child is Born	Johnny Mathis

(Both on general release)

Dance tapes and instructions available from:
Hugh Sprigg
27 Osberton Place
Sheffield s11 8AL
England

and

Dancing Circles
Wesley Cottage
New Road
East Huntspill
Highbridge
Somerset TA9 3PT

Books

Under the Eye of the Clock, Christopher Nolan, Weidenfeld & Nicholson

A Step Further, Joni Eareckson, Zondervan

Jonathan Livingston Seagull, Richard Bach, Pan

The Diary of Anne Frank, Pan

Dreams Alive: Prayers by Teenagers, ed. Carl Koch, St Mary's Press

More Parables & Fables, Peter Ribes SJ, St Pauls

Patrick Kavanagh's Collected Poems, Gallery Press

I am David, Anne Holm, Magnet

The Little Prince, Antoine de St Exupéry, Mammoth